Mystic Love

Exploring Sexual Magic and Spiritual Intimacy

Alex Johnson

© Copyright 2024 - All rights reserved.

The content contained within this book may not be reproduced, duplicated or transmitted without direct written permission from the author or the publisher.

Under no circumstances will any blame or legal responsibility be held against the publisher, or author, for any damages, reparation, or monetary loss due to the information contained within this book, either directly or indirectly.

Legal Notice:

This book is copyright protected. It is only for personal use. You cannot amend, distribute, sell, use, quote or paraphrase any part, or the content within this book, without the consent of the author or publisher.

Disclaimer Notice:

Please note the information contained within this document is for educational and entertainment purposes only. All effort has been executed to present accurate, up to date, reliable, complete information. No warranties of any kind are declared or implied. Readers acknowledge that the author is not engaging in the rendering of legal, financial, medical or professional advice. The content within this book has been derived from various sources. Please consult a licensed professional before attempting any techniques outlined in this book.

By reading this document, the reader agrees that under no circumstances is the author responsible for any losses, direct or indirect, that are incurred as a result of the use of information contained within this document, including, but not limited to, errors, omissions, or inaccuracies.

Table of Contents

INTRODUCTION 6

CHAPTER I. Understanding Sexual Magic 9

    Defining Sexual Magic: Origins and Concepts 9

    Historical Perspectives on Sexual Magic 12

    Modern Interpretations and Applications 15

    Ethical Considerations and Cultural Variances 18

CHAPTER II. The Spiritual Dimension of Intimacy 22

    Exploring Spiritual Intimacy in Relationships 22

    Connection Between Sexuality and Spirituality 25

    Sacred Sexuality Practices from Different Cultures 28

    How Spirituality Enhances Intimate Relationships 31

CHAPTER III. Unlocking Mystical Powers Within 35

    Harnessing Energy Through Tantra 35

    The Power of Rituals and Symbolism in Sexual Magic .. 38

    Meditation and Visualization Techniques for Spiritual Connection 41

    Awakening Kundalini Energy for Spiritual Growth 44

CHAPTER IV. Healing and Transformation Through Sexual Magic 49

    Healing Trauma and Blockages Through Sacred Sexuality 49

    Overcoming Shame and Guilt Surrounding Sexuality ... 53

    Using Sexual Energy for Personal and Spiritual Growth 56

Case Studies and Success Stories 59

CHAPTER V. Deepening Connection Through Rituals and Practices 63

Rituals for Enhancing Intimacy and Connection 63

Sacred Sexuality Practices for Couples 66

Exploring Sacred Union and Divine Partnership 69

Integrating Spiritual Practices into Daily Life 73

CHAPTER VI. Challenges and Pitfalls in Spiritual Intimacy 76

Addressing Common Misconceptions and Challenges . 76

Navigating Differences in Sexual Desire and Spiritual Beliefs 79

Overcoming Cultural and Religious Barriers 82

Maintaining Boundaries and Consent in Spiritual Relationships 85

CHAPTER VII. Embracing Love, Pleasure, and Spirituality 89

Cultivating Love and Compassion in Sexual Relationships 89

Finding Pleasure and Joy in Spiritual Intimacy 92

Balancing Physical and Spiritual Needs 95

Embracing Self-Love and Self-Care Practices 98

CHAPTER VIII. The Future of Sexual Magic and Spiritual Intimacy 102

Trends and Innovations in Sacred Sexuality Practices 102

Integrating Technology and Tradition in Spiritual Connection 105

Building Communities and Support Networks for Spiritual Intimacy... 108

Personal Reflections and Looking Forward 111

CHAPTER IX. Reflection **116**

Recapitulation of Key Concepts and Insights 116

Final Thoughts on the Journey of Exploring Mystic Love 119

Encouragement for Further Exploration and Growth . 122

CONCLUSION **126**

INTRODUCTION

In the vast tapestry of human experience, few realms captivate the imagination and stir the soul as deeply as the interconnected realms of sexuality and spirituality. For millennia, these two forces have been revered, explored, and intertwined across diverse cultures and belief systems in the pursuit of deeper understanding, personal growth, and transcendent union. In "Mystic Love: Exploring Sexual Magic and Spiritual Intimacy," we embark on a journey to delve into the profound connection between sexual expression and spiritual awakening, inviting readers to explore the rich landscapes of mystic love.

In this introductory chapter, we set the stage for our exploration by illuminating the significance of this union and providing an overview of the themes and concepts that will guide our journey. We delve into the origins of sexual magic and spiritual intimacy, tracing their historical roots and examining their modern interpretations. Through this exploration, we seek to uncover the transformative potential inherent in embracing sexuality as a path to spiritual growth and intimate connection.

At the heart of our inquiry lies the concept of sexual magic—a practice steeped in mystery and ancient wisdom. Defined as the conscious use of sexual energy for spiritual purposes, sexual magic has been a cornerstone of esoteric traditions throughout history. From the tantric practices of ancient India to the rituals of Western occultism, sexual magic has been regarded as a potent tool for unlocking the hidden depths of human potential and forging a profound connection with the divine.

Yet, sexual magic is not merely a relic of bygone eras; it is a living tradition that continues to evolve and thrive in the modern world. In recent decades, there has been a resurgence of interest in sacred sexuality and tantra, as individuals seek to reclaim their sexual sovereignty and explore the depths of their spiritual nature. This resurgence has been fueled by a rising recognition of the limitations of traditional methods to sexuality, which often overlook the profound spiritual dimensions of human intimacy.

Central to our exploration of sexual magic is the concept of spiritual intimacy—the deep, soulful connection that arises when two individuals come together in love and trust. Unlike mere physical intimacy, which may be fleeting or superficial, spiritual intimacy transcends the boundaries of the ego, allowing us to experience a sense of oneness with our partner and with the divine. Through spiritual intimacy, we can tap into the transformative power of love and sexuality, using them as vehicles for personal healing, growth, and awakening.

As we embark on this journey together, it is essential to acknowledge that the path of mystic love is not always easy. Along the way, we may encounter obstacles and challenges that test our resolve and also push us to confront our deepest fears as well as insecurities. Yet, it is precisely through these challenges that we have the opportunity to grow and evolve, deepening our understanding of ourselves and our connection to the world around us.

In the following pages, we will explore various topics related to sexual magic and spiritual intimacy, from the ancient wisdom of tantra to the latest trends in modern spirituality. We will delve into practical techniques and exercises designed to help you cultivate a more profound connection with your own sexuality and spirituality, as well as with your partner(s). We will also assess the ethical considerations and cultural variances that shape our understanding of these practices, ensuring that our exploration is grounded in respect, integrity, and compassion.

Ultimately, our goal is not merely to impart knowledge or offer solutions, but to inspire you to embark on your own journey of self-discovery and transformation. Whether you are a seasoned practitioner or a curious seeker, "Mystic Love" invites you to explore the limitless opportunities that arise when we embrace the union of sexuality and spirituality—a journey that promises to be both challenging and rewarding but, above all, deeply enriching.

CHAPTER I

Understanding Sexual Magic

Defining Sexual Magic: Origins and Concepts

Sexual magic, a subject shrouded in mystery and often relegated to the fringes of esoteric studies, intertwines the potent forces of sexuality and spirituality. This section delves into the origins and concepts of sexual magic, exploring its historical roots and the various philosophical and practical dimensions that characterize this intriguing practice.

The origins of sexual magic trace back to ancient civilizations, where the union of sexuality and spirituality was seen not as taboo, but as a vital aspect of religious and mystical experience. In ancient Egypt, for instance, the creation myths involving Isis and Osiris prominently feature sexual themes, symbolizing regeneration and the cyclical nature of life and death. These stories underscored the belief that sexual union possessed the power to bridge the earthly and the divine, a foundational concept in sexual magic.

Similarly, in Eastern traditions, particularly within Tantric practices of Hinduism and Buddhism, sexual activity transcends its physical dimensions to assume a sacramental role. Tantra, which means "to weave" in Sanskrit, integrates sexuality into spiritual practice, aiming to elevate life force or 'kundalini' energy through the chakras (energy centers of the body) to achieve enlightenment. The sexual act, in Tantric philosophy, is revered not only for pleasure or procreation but as a profound means of spiritual advancement and connection with the divine.

In the Western esoteric tradition, sexual magic emerged more explicitly with the rise of occult movements in the late 19th and early 20th centuries. Figures such as Paschal Beverly Randolph, an American occultist and spiritualist, pioneered the practice of sexual magic in the West. He posited that sexual union, when executed with specific magical intentions, could initiate profound mystical experiences and tangible magical outcomes. Randolph's work laid the groundwork for later occultists, including Aleister Crowley, who further developed these ideas within the context of Thelema, his philosophical and religious system. Crowley's interpretation of sexual magic was heavily influenced by his belief in the maxim "Do what thou wilt," which he connected to the pursuit of one's true will, often facilitated through magical practices, including sexual rituals.

The core concept of sexual magic revolves around the idea that sexual energy, when harnessed and directed through ritual, can be a powerful tool for spiritual growth and manifestation. This energy, considered the primal life force, can be used to enhance personal power, forge psychic connections, or manifest specific outcomes in the physical world. The practices typically involve more than just the act of sex; they include a variety of ritualistic elements such as meditation, invocation of deities, and specific magical operations intended to focus and direct the energy generated during sexual activity.

Philosophically, sexual magic is underpinned by the principle of polarity. This principle posits that dual forces govern the universe, often conceptualized as masculine and feminine energies. In sexual magic, the union of these energies, through the sexual act, is seen as a microcosmic reflection of the cosmic balance of forces. This union is believed to generate a unique metaphysical energy that can initiate spiritual transformation and magical manifestation.

Critically, sexual magic is not without its controversies and misconceptions. It has been often misunderstood and misrepresented in popular culture, leading to associations with hedonism and moral decay. However, within the practices themselves, there is a strong emphasis on consent, sacredness, and the ethical use of magical power. Practitioners of sexual magic typically stress the importance of intention, boundaries, and the spiritual growth of all involved.

The modern revival and interest in sexual magic reflect a broader cultural shift towards recognizing and integrating sexuality as a vital aspect of spiritual and personal development. Contemporary practitioners continue to explore and adapt these ancient practices, often integrating modern psychological insights and feminist perspectives, which challenge traditional gender roles and power dynamics inherent in some historical practices.

In conclusion, sexual magic represents a complex and rich field of esoteric practice that has evolved significantly over millennia. From its origins in ancient mythologies to its recontextualization in modern occult practices, it has consistently highlighted the profound connection between sexuality and the spiritual realm. As contemporary seekers continue to explore and adapt sexual magic, they uncover new layers of meaning and potential, reinforcing its place as a powerful tool in the quest for spiritual insight and transformation. This ongoing evolution ensures that sexual magic remains a dynamic and evolving path of spiritual inquiry, ripe with potential for personal and collective empowerment.

Historical Perspectives on Sexual Magic

Sexual magic, often veiled in secrecy and mystique, possesses a long and complex history that intertwines with the evolution of human spirituality and esoteric traditions. This section explores the historical perspectives on sexual magic, tracing its development through various cultures and epochs, and examining its philosophical underpinnings and practices.

The concept of sexual magic—or the use of sexual acts and energies for magical or spiritual purposes—finds its roots in the earliest human civilizations. Ancient texts and artifacts from societies such as the Sumerians, Egyptians, and Indians suggest that the act of creation, both physical and metaphysical, was inherently linked to sexuality. These cultures recognized sexual union as a potent source of life force energy, capable of influencing the spiritual realm and effecting change in the material world. For instance, the Sumerian myth of Inanna and Dumuzi explicitly celebrates their sexual union, highlighting the fertility and prosperity it brings to the land. Such narratives underscore the sacredness attributed to sexual acts, positioning them as vital components of ritual and ceremony.

In Ancient Egypt, sexual magic was embedded within the fabric of religious practice. The pharaohs, considered divine beings, engaged in ritualistic sexual acts with priestesses, believed to ensure the flooding of the Nile and the fertility of the land. The Osirian myth, involving Isis's resurrection of Osiris and their posthumous conjugal union, symbolizes the regenerative power of sexual love, underscoring the belief in sexuality as a conduit to divine power and eternal life.

The Eastern traditions, particularly Tantra, offer perhaps the most sophisticated historical perspective on sexual magic. Originating in medieval India, Tantric practices encompass a wide range of spiritual teachings and rituals that view the body as a temple and sexuality as a path to enlightenment. Unlike Western views that often dichotomize spirit and flesh, Tantra sees the sexual and the spiritual as intricately connected. Through rituals involving sexual union, known as Maithuna, practitioners aim to awaken the Kundalini energy and achieve a state of divine union and consciousness expansion. These practices underscore the integration of sexuality into spiritual and mystical pursuits, emphasizing the transformational potential of sexual energy.

The Western esoteric tradition, particularly from the medieval period onwards, presents a more cautious approach to sexual magic. While acknowledging the potent force of sexual energy, many Western magical traditions often surrounded sexual magic with warnings and restrictions, reflecting broader societal taboos around sexuality. However, the Renaissance brought a renewed interest in ancient philosophies and esoteric practices, including those involving sexuality. The works of figures such as Giordano Bruno and Heinrich Cornelius Agrippa began to explore the connections between sexuality, magic, and the cosmos, albeit often in veiled language.

The modern era witnessed a significant resurgence of interest in sexual magic, particularly within the context of the occult revival of the late 19th and early 20th centuries. Figures such as Paschal Beverly Randolph, Aleister Crowley, and later, Gerald Gardner, integrated sexual magical practices into their teachings and rituals. Randolph, an African American spiritualist and occultist, was among the first to explicitly articulate the principles of sexual magic in the Western context, advocating its use for spiritual enlightenment and magical work. Crowley, perhaps one of the most infamous figures associated with sexual magic, emphasized the transgressive and liberating aspects of sexual magical practices, advocating their use as a means of achieving Thelema's central tenet: the pursuit of one's True Will.

The 20th century also saw the rise of neo-pagan and feminist spiritual movements, which embraced sexual magic as a form of empowerment and a means of reconnecting with ancient, goddess-centered religions. These movements, including Wicca and various forms of witchcraft, often emphasize the sacredness of sexuality and its role in connecting with the divine, celebrating the body and sexual pleasure as aspects of spiritual practice.

Throughout its history, sexual magic has been characterized by a tension between its recognition as a potent spiritual practice and societal taboos surrounding sexuality. This tension has led to a complex legacy, where sexual magical practices have often been shrouded in secrecy, misunderstood, or maligned. However, historical perspectives on sexual magic reveal a rich tapestry of beliefs and practices that recognize the profound connection between sexuality and the spiritual realm.

In examining the historical perspectives on sexual magic, it is clear that this practice has served as a powerful means of exploring the mysteries of life, creation, and spiritual transformation. From the fertility rites of ancient civilizations to the sophisticated rituals of Tantric practitioners and the esoteric explorations of modern occultists, sexual magic has been a dynamic and evolving aspect of human spiritual practice. Despite the challenges and controversies it has faced, the historical journey of sexual magic underscores humanity's enduring quest to understand the sacred nature of sexuality and its potential to unlock deeper spiritual truths.

As we continue to explore the intersections of sexuality and spirituality, the historical perspectives on sexual magic offer valuable insights into how human societies have sought to harness sexual energies for spiritual growth and transformation. This exploration not only enriches our understanding of past practices but also informs contemporary discussions about the place of sexuality in spiritual and magical practices today. In this context, sexual magic remains a compelling and provocative field, promising further insights and developments as scholars and practitioners continue to delve into its mysteries and potentials.

Modern Interpretations and Applications

Sexual magic, an ancient esoteric practice that harnesses the transformative power of sexual energy for spiritual and material purposes, has evolved significantly over the centuries. In the contemporary era, these practices have been revisited and adapted to modern sensibilities, reflecting changes in societal attitudes towards sexuality and spirituality. This section explores the modern interpretations and applications of sexual magic, examining its integration into new age movements, its psychological dimensions, and the ethical considerations it entails.

Modern interpretations of sexual magic are deeply influenced by the revival of occult and pagan traditions in the 20th century, particularly through figures like Aleister Crowley, who redefined sexual magic in the context of Thelema. Crowley's writings emphasized the sacramental nature of sexual acts and introduced the concept of using sexual energy as a means of achieving one's True Will, an idea that has profoundly impacted contemporary magical practices. His approach was not merely about the physical aspects of sex but about the alchemical transformation it could engender within the practitioner, elevating the act to a metaphysical plane.

Following Crowley, the rise of neo-pagan and Wiccan traditions in the mid-20th century further facilitated the mainstreaming of sexual magic. These traditions often celebrate sexuality as a powerful force that is both sacred and integral to spiritual growth. In these contexts, sexual magic is frequently linked with natural cycles and rites of fertility, emphasizing a holistic connection between the body, nature, and the divine. Gerald Gardner, the founder of Wicca, incorporated elements of sexual magic into his teachings, albeit more implicitly, focusing on the creative and bonding powers of sexual rites.

In the contemporary spiritual landscape, sexual magic has also been influenced by Eastern philosophies, particularly Tantra, which many Western seekers have embraced. Unlike traditional Western views that often portray sexuality in opposition to spiritual purity, Tantra offers a path where sexual expressions are viewed as a means to spiritual enlightenment. This synthesis has led to a version of sexual magic that is both a practice of pleasure and a profound spiritual journey, aiming to dissolve the illusions of ego and unite with the cosmic consciousness.

Psychologically, modern sexual magic has been explored through the lens of Jungian psychology, which interprets these practices as methods for accessing the collective unconscious and integrating disparate aspects of the self. Jung's concepts of the anima and animus, representations of the feminine and masculine energies within each individual, parallel the sexual magical emphasis on the union of opposite forces to achieve wholeness and psychic balance. Practitioners often use sexual magic rituals as tools for psychological healing, seeing them as ways to address deep-seated issues and to foster intimacy and understanding between partners.

The practical applications of sexual magic in modern times are diverse, ranging from personal transformation and healing to the attainment of specific outcomes, such as the manifestation of desires or the creation of magical talismans. These practices generally involve rituals that create a sacred space, the use of specific symbols and incantations, and the deliberate channeling of sexual energy towards the intended purpose. Such rituals underscore the belief in the power of intention and the efficacy of combining sexual energy with magical practices.

Ethically, the modern practice of sexual magic faces significant scrutiny. The issues of consent, power dynamics, and the potential for exploitation are critically crucial in practices that combine sexuality with spiritual authority. Contemporary practitioners are increasingly aware of these concerns and often emphasize ethical standards, including clear communication, consent, and mutual respect among participants. The integration of feminist and egalitarian ideals into sexual magic practices is also a feature of modern interpretations, challenging traditional gender roles and seeking to empower all participants.

Furthermore, the modern discourse around sexual magic includes a greater acknowledgment of its therapeutic potential. Some practitioners integrate elements of sex therapy and psychological counseling with sexual magical practices, aiming to heal sexual traumas and enhance relational dynamics. This therapeutic approach is seen not only as a way to enrich personal and spiritual life but also as a means of restoring the sacredness of sexuality as a fundamental aspect of human experience.

As sexual magic continues to evolve, it increasingly interacts with other movements such as the LGBTQ+ community, which explores these practices within a framework that challenges heteronormative assumptions and expands the definitions of sexual and spiritual expressions. This inclusive approach not only broadens the scope of sexual magic but also enriches it, offering new perspectives and possibilities for transformation.

In conclusion, modern interpretations and applications of sexual magic reflect a complex and evolving landscape where ancient traditions meet contemporary spiritual and ethical insights. The practice of sexual magic today is marked by a profound respect for the power of sexuality as a transformative force, balanced by a mindful approach to ethical issues and psychological health. As society continues to evolve in its understanding of sexuality and spirituality, the practices of sexual magic are likely to expand and diversify, offering rich possibilities for personal and collective growth. This ongoing evolution makes sexual magic a vibrant and dynamic field, capable of significant impact in the realms of spirituality, therapy, and personal empowerment.

Ethical Considerations and Cultural Variances

Sexual magic, a complex facet of esoteric traditions, harnesses the profound energies of sexual acts to achieve spiritual enlightenment and material manifestations. This practice, however, raises significant ethical considerations and exhibits notable cultural variances that merit careful examination. This section explores these ethical dilemmas and the cultural differences in the practice of sexual magic, providing a comprehensive overview of its impact and the precautions necessary to navigate its sensitive nature.

The ethical landscape of sexual magic is fraught with challenges, primarily due to the intimate and potent nature of sexual energy. At the heart of these ethical considerations is the principle of consent. Consent in sexual magic must be informed, enthusiastic, and continuous, which means all parties must have a clear understanding of the ritual's purposes, potential impacts, and the ability to withdraw at any time. This is especially critical in a practice that combines profound emotional, physical, and spiritual interactions, which can lead to complex power dynamics.

Another major ethical concern is the potential for abuse of power. Sexual magic often occurs within the context of a hierarchical structure, such as between a teacher and student or a leader and a group member. In such settings, the risk of coercion can be significant. Thus, Ethical practice requires clear boundaries and the avoidance of manipulative behaviors that could influence personal autonomy. Transparency regarding the intentions and methods used in rituals and the aftercare for all participants is essential to maintain ethical integrity.

Confidentiality is another cornerstone of ethical sexual magic practice. Participants must be able to trust that their experiences and identities will be protected, particularly as the stigma surrounding such practices can expose individuals to social ostracism or discrimination. Therefore, practitioners need to ensure that privacy is upheld and that the personal information disclosed during rituals is treated with the utmost discretion.

Sexual magic is not a monolithic practice but varies significantly across different cultures and spiritual traditions. These variances can be seen in the practices' purposes, methods, and the roles of participants, which are often deeply influenced by broader cultural beliefs and values.

In Western traditions, particularly within modern Pagan and Thelemic communities, sexual magic is frequently associated with personal empowerment and spiritual evolution. It is often practiced in a ritualistic context, with a strong emphasis on individual consent and the magical intention of achieving one's True Will, as popularized by Aleister Crowley. The practices may include elaborate rites, using symbols, oils, and invocations to direct energy towards specific goals.

Contrastingly, in Eastern traditions, particularly within Tantra, sexual magic (or Maithuna) is seen as a means to transcend the self and achieve union with the divine. This practice involves more than just the physical act of sex; it is a spiritual exercise that incorporates meditation, breath control, and ritual to harness sexual energy. The emphasis is on spiritual enlightenment rather than on personal or materialistic outcomes.

Indigenous practices also provide a rich tapestry of sexual magic. For example, in particular South American tribal cultures, sexual rites are integrated into broader healing ceremonies that involve the entire community. These practices often focus on the healing power of sexual energy and its ability to restore balance and harmony to individuals and the group at large.

Integrating ethical practices in sexual magic is critical to address these challenges effectively. This includes the development of frameworks that ensure all activities are consensual, respectful, and confidential. Practitioners and participants should be educated about the ethical dimensions of sexual magic, including the importance of consent and the potential psychological impacts of the rituals.

Training and guidelines for practitioners can also help mitigate the risks associated with power dynamics. This might include certifications or ethical codes developed by community leaders or organizations that outline best practices and provide recourse for those who may experience abuse. Additionally, the role of community oversight cannot be underestimated; a community-regulated approach can help maintain high ethical standards and provide a support network for participants.

In conclusion, sexual magic is a deeply complex practice enriched by its cultural diversity and challenged by significant ethical considerations. The practice necessitates a careful approach to consent, power dynamics, and confidentiality to safeguard the well-being of all participants. Meanwhile, understanding the cultural contexts and variances of sexual magic can provide valuable insights into its practices and help foster respect and integrity within its communities. As interest in esoteric and pagan traditions continues to grow, so does the need for an ethical framework that respects both the power and the potential of sexual magic. This framework must be adaptable to different cultural understandings and sensitive to the vulnerabilities of this profound practice. In navigating these waters, the global community of sexual magic practitioners can ensure that their pursuits are not only effective but also ethical and respectful of the diverse landscapes in which they operate.

CHAPTER II

The Spiritual Dimension of Intimacy

Exploring Spiritual Intimacy in Relationships

Spiritual intimacy in relationships is a profound connection that transcends the physical and emotional aspects, fostering a deep, shared sense of meaning and purpose between partners. This form of intimacy involves the mutual exploration of beliefs, the nurturing of a shared spiritual path, and the support of each individual's personal growth within a spiritual framework. This section delves into the concept of spiritual intimacy, examining its significance, the methods through which it can be cultivated, and the impact it has on relationships.

The idea that our relationships can be a conduit for spiritual growth is at the core of spiritual intimacy. Partners who engage in spiritual intimacy often find that their relationship becomes a reflective space for understanding life's deeper meanings and for addressing existential questions in a supportive and understanding environment. This goes beyond traditional religious practices and includes a broader, more inclusive exploration of spirituality that can accommodate diverse beliefs and practices.

The significance of spiritual intimacy lies in its ability to enrich relationships by adding a layer of depth that other forms of intimacy might not reach. This depth comes from a shared pursuit of life's ultimate questions and a mutual respect for the sacred—however it may be defined by the couple. Whether partners follow the same spiritual path or explore different traditions, the respect and curiosity they bring to these discussions can significantly enhance mutual understanding and compassion.

Cultivating spiritual intimacy requires deliberate efforts by both partners. It begins with open communication about one's spiritual beliefs, desires, and experiences. This dialogue should be characterized by openness and vulnerability, with each partner willing to share and listen without judgment. Such discussions can include topics like the impact of spiritual beliefs on daily life, personal experiences with the divine, or how spiritual teachings can inform relationship dynamics and personal growth.

Practical methods for cultivating spiritual intimacy include shared rituals, meditation, prayer, study, or participating in spiritual communities together. These practices can help synchronize spiritual rhythms through joint participation and reflection. For instance, couples might choose to meditate together each morning, attend spiritual services, go on retreats designed to enhance spiritual understanding, or simply read and discuss spiritual texts that resonate with them.

The benefits of spiritual intimacy extend beyond the personal as well as spiritual growth of the individuals involved. It also enhances relational dynamics. For example, couples who share spiritual intimacy typically exhibit higher levels of trust and cooperation, as they often align on core values and visions for their life together. This alignment can significantly reduce conflict and enhance the resilience of the relationship, making it better equipped to handle the challenges that come with life's inevitable fluctuations.

Moreover, spiritual intimacy can lead to greater emotional intimacy, as the practices involved often cultivate qualities like empathy, patience, and unconditional love. These qualities are essential for deep emotional connections and can help partners support each other through personal and shared challenges. Furthermore, this type of intimacy promotes a holistic understanding of each partner, recognizing them as complex beings with spiritual, physical, emotional, and mental dimensions.

However, cultivating spiritual intimacy is not without its challenges. Differences in spiritual beliefs can be a source of conflict, especially if one partner feels superior about their spiritual path or if one partner is less interested in exploring spirituality than the other. To navigate such differences, couples must maintain an attitude of respect and curiosity about each other's beliefs rather than judgment. This can involve establishing boundaries around spiritual discussions, finding common ground, or agreeing to disagree respectfully.

Another challenge is the risk of co-dependency, where one or both partners might become overly reliant on the relationship for their spiritual fulfillment. Each partner can mitigate this by maintaining their own spiritual practices and identities, which can enrich the shared spiritual journey by bringing diverse experiences and insights to the relationship.

In conclusion, spiritual intimacy offers a unique and enriching relationship dimension that can foster profound personal growth and enhance relational dynamics. By engaging in open dialogue, sharing spiritual practices, and supporting each other's spiritual paths, couples can develop a deep, meaningful connection that strengthens their relationship. While challenges may arise, particularly when navigating differences in spiritual beliefs or avoiding co-dependency, these can be addressed through respectful communication and a commitment to mutual growth. Ultimately, exploring spiritual intimacy allows couples to grow together and help each other evolve into their fullest selves, enriching their relationship and individual lives.

Connection Between Sexuality and Spirituality

The relationship between sexuality and spirituality has been a subject of contemplation and scholarly discussion for centuries. These two fundamental aspects of human experience are often viewed through separate lenses; however, many philosophical and religious traditions suggest a profound connection between them. This section explores the intricate link between sexuality and spirituality, examining how this connection is perceived across different cultures, the implications of their convergence, and the transformative potential inherent in integrating these aspects of human life.

Sexuality and spirituality are both intrinsic to the human condition, involving powerful energies that drive personal and collective existence. Spirituality often relates to seeking meaning, connecting with the transcendent, and experiencing a deep sense of aliveness and interconnectedness with all beings. Sexuality, on the other hand, encompasses the biological, erotic, and intimate dimensions of human relationships that foster connection, procreation, and pleasure. Despite their apparent differences, these two dimensions are deeply interwoven, with each capable of enhancing and enriching the understanding of the other.

Historically, many religious traditions have prescribed strict guidelines regarding sexual behavior, often with the aim of spiritual refinement. For instance, in several branches of Christianity, celibacy is revered as a higher spiritual calling that signifies purity and control over base desires. Conversely, Eastern traditions such as Hinduism and Buddhism acknowledge a more integral relationship between sexuality and spirituality. In these cultures, sexual expression is often seen not just as a part of human nature but as a potential pathway to spiritual enlightenment. The Tantric traditions of Hinduism and Vajrayana Buddhism, for example, utilize sexual symbolism and practices as metaphors and means for spiritual advancement, suggesting that sexual union can mirror the union of the divine and the mortal.

In the realm of Tantra, which is perhaps the most well-known spiritual tradition emphasizing the sacredness of sexuality, sexual acts are framed as rituals that have the potential to transcend personal limitations. Here, sexuality is a sacred act capable of dissolving the illusion of separation between self and other, leading to a profound experience of oneness with all existence. This practice is not about hedonism but is a disciplined form of meditation that uses all aspects of human experience, including sexuality, as avenues to spiritual realization.

Similarly, the indigenous spiritual systems of many tribal societies also reflect a nuanced understanding of the sexuality-spirituality nexus. For these cultures, life force energy—often directly linked to sexual energy—is considered a critical element of spiritual and physical health. Rituals that involve expressions of sexuality are, therefore, not merely about societal rites but deeply spiritual undertakings that promote harmony, fertility, and well-being within the community.

In contemporary times, the exploration of the connection between sexuality and spirituality has been influenced by the psychological theories of figures like Carl Jung, who introduced the idea of the 'anima' and 'animus' as the feminine and masculine dimensions present within each individual. Jungian thought suggests that true psychological and spiritual maturity involves the integration of these aspects within oneself, which can be facilitated through exploring one's sexuality in a conscious, reflective manner. This perspective has been further expanded upon by modern psychologists and spiritual teachers who view sexual energy as a powerful force for personal transformation and healing.

The practical implications of combining sexuality and spirituality are profound. On a personal level, integrating these aspects can lead to a more holistic self-understanding and a more fulfilling sense of intimacy with oneself and others. In a relational context, this integration often results in deeper connections that are not only physical but also emotional and spiritual. For many, this holistic approach to sexuality can lead to greater creativity, vitality, and a sense of peace, indicative of spiritual growth.

However, the path to integrating sexuality and spirituality is not devoid of challenges. Societal norms and personal beliefs often impose barriers that can make this integration difficult. For example, pervasive cultural narratives that view sexual expression as inherently sinful or shameful can lead to conflicts between one's natural sexual desires and their spiritual beliefs. Overcoming these dichotomies requires a reevaluation of both the societal attitudes towards sexuality and the personal internalization of these attitudes.

Moreover, the journey towards integrating these dimensions can also surface personal vulnerabilities and wounds associated with sexuality, such as past traumas or negative experiences. Addressing these issues often necessitates a process of healing and forgiveness that can be both painful and liberating. Nevertheless, many find that engaging in this process contributes to personal and spiritual growth and enhances their relational dynamics, leading to more meaningful and compassionate partnerships.

In conclusion, the connection between sexuality and spirituality is complex and multifaceted, reflecting deep layers of human experience. While historically seen through divergent or even opposing lenses, there is a growing recognition of their profound interconnection. This recognition is fostering new understandings and practices that embrace the totality of human experience, offering pathways to greater fulfillment and transformation. As more individuals and cultures explore this connection, the potential for a more integrated, holistic approach to living becomes increasingly apparent. This exploration promises to enrich individual lives and foster a more compassionate, understanding, and spiritually aware society.

Sacred Sexuality Practices from Different Cultures

Sacred sexuality encompasses a variety of practices where sexual activities are integrated with religious or spiritual rituals, often aiming to transcend ordinary experience to achieve a deeper, spiritual connection. This section explores the rich tapestry of sacred sexuality practices across different cultures, from ancient rites to contemporary applications, and how these practices reflect broader spiritual and cultural paradigms.

In Ancient Egypt, sexuality was deeply integrated into their mythology and religious practices. For example, the cult of Isis and Osiris centered around the themes of death, resurrection, and fertility, with sexual union playing a crucial role in Osiris's resurrection and the subsequent assurance of the Nile's fertility. These myths were reenacted through ceremonial plays and were believed to harness sexual energy to promote fertility and life force, essential for both agriculture and human procreation. The practices around these deities suggest a culture where sexuality and spirituality were closely intertwined, reflecting an integrated view of the divine in everyday life.

Perhaps the most detailed and structured approach to sacred sexuality can be found in Tantra, a branch of Hindu and Buddhist traditions. Unlike the often repressive attitudes toward sex seen in many Western spiritual traditions, Tantra views sexual union as a powerful path to enlightenment. The Maithuna ritual, or sexual union in Tantra, is considered a sacred act capable of elevating its participants above mere physical union, symbolizing the joining of divine feminine and masculine energies. Through controlled, ritualistic practices involving mantras, mudras, and yantras, participants aim to harness the creative powers of the universe itself. This ritual is not just about physical pleasure but about using that pleasure as a means to spiritual transcendence and enlightenment.

In many indigenous African cultures, sexuality and spirituality are not viewed as separate but are part of a holistic understanding of life. Rituals that emphasize fertility and vitality often include sexual elements, which are considered sacred. For instance, in certain Ndebele tribes, rites of passage into adulthood include teachings and rituals that incorporate sexual knowledge, which is crucial for the tribe's vitality. These practices are not hidden but are celebrated as significant communal events, highlighting the community's role in guiding spiritual and sexual maturation.

In Native American cultures, the integration of sexuality and spirituality can be seen in various symbolic rituals and teachings. The Two-Spirit tradition, in particular, embodies this integration deeply. Two-Spirit individuals—often revered within their tribes—were believed to hold both feminine and masculine spirits, which allowed them to transcend traditional gender roles and mediate between the physical and spiritual worlds. Sexual union, within or involving Two-Spirit individuals, was seen not merely as a physical act but as a spiritual interface, where physical boundaries dissolved, and spiritual insight could be achieved.

In Shinto, Japan's indigenous spirituality, sexual symbols and rituals play a prominent role. Certain Shinto rituals are designed to ensure fertility and prosperity, linking the energy of sexual union with agricultural abundance. Meanwhile, Daoism in China introduces the concept of dual cultivation, where sexual practices are used to harmonize and balance one's internal male and female energies. These practices are believed to promote health, longevity, and spiritual insight, reflecting an intrinsic belief in the health-spirituality nexus.

In modern practices such as Wicca and broader Neo-Paganism, sexuality is often celebrated as a powerful force connected to nature and spirituality. Rituals, including the Great Rite, explicitly use sexual acts or their symbolic representations to embody the union between the goddess and the god, celebrating and harnessing fertility and the life force. These rituals are typically performed with a deep sense of the sacred and often involve a consensual exchange of energy intended to elevate consciousness and communion with nature.

The application of sacred sexuality in modern times comes with a heightened awareness of ethical considerations. Consent and respect are paramount, as these practices often involve intimate and vulnerable experiences. Modern practitioners are increasingly incorporating ethical guidelines to ensure that sacred sexuality is practiced in ways that honor personal boundaries and integrity.

Moreover, contemporary interpretations of sacred sexuality often involve elements of psychotherapy and healing, recognizing the potential for sexual energy to heal and restore psychological and spiritual wellness. This is evident in practices such as tantric therapy and spiritual sex counseling, which integrate traditional spiritual teachings with modern psychological insights.

In conclusion, sacred sexuality practices from different cultures illustrate a universal recognition of the profound link between sexual and spiritual energies. While the specific practices and beliefs vary widely, they all reflect a common understanding that sexuality can transcend its physical dimensions to become a powerful vehicle for spiritual enlightenment, community cohesion, and personal transformation. These practices remind us of the potential to treat sexual experiences as sacred, transformative, and deeply connected to the spiritual fabric of life. As we continue to explore and integrate these ancient wisdoms into contemporary practices, we can redefine and enrich our understanding of spirituality and sexuality in profound and life-affirming ways.

How Spirituality Enhances Intimate Relationships

Spirituality often transforms intimate relationships by offering depth and a shared sense of purpose that can significantly enhance them. This section explores the various dimensions through which spirituality enriches intimate relationships, examining its impact on communication, conflict resolution, mutual growth, and connection to a broader existential understanding.

One of the primary ways in which spirituality enhances intimate relationships is by improving communication. Spiritual practices often emphasize the values of honesty, openness, and authenticity, encouraging individuals to share their true selves. In the context of an intimate relationship, such spiritual values foster a communication style that is deeply empathetic, notably more reflective, and inherently compassionate. This type of communication is vital for building trust and understanding between partners, permitting them to express their needs, fears, and desires without judgment. Moreover, spiritual traditions often advocate for mindful listening, which involves hearing words and empathizing with the emotional undertones of a partner's speech. This holistic approach to communication can transform interactions in a relationship, making them richer and more meaningful.

Conflict is known as a natural aspect of any relationship, but the way it is handled can determine the health as well as longevity of a partnership. Spirituality can play a crucial role in conflict resolution by providing a framework that promotes forgiveness, patience, and humility. These virtues help individuals to transcend their egos and address conflicts from a place of love and understanding rather than retaliation. Furthermore, many spiritual teachings include meditative practices that enhance self-awareness. This heightened self-awareness enables individuals to recognize their contributions to conflicts and differentiate between their emotions and their true selves, which is essential for resolving disputes calmly and constructively.

Spirituality can encourage partners to support each other's personal and spiritual growth, creating a dynamic relationship that evolves over time. This aspect of spirituality in relationships involves recognizing the journey each partner is on and understanding that each path may require different things at different times. It's about nurturing the soil in which both partners can grow—not necessarily always in unison, but always with mutual support. Such an environment not only strengthens the relationship but also enriches the individual lives of each partner, allowing them to flourish in all dimensions of their being. Additionally, when both partners are committed to their own spiritual growth, they bring new insights and energies into the relationship, preventing stagnation and imbuing the relationship with ongoing vitality and curiosity.

One of the most profound ways spirituality enhances intimate relationships is by creating shared meaning and purpose. Couples who engage in spiritual practices together or even separately but with a shared spiritual understanding often find that these practices help them construct a larger life framework. This might involve shared goals, values, or a mutual commitment to service or ethical living. Such shared meaning binds the couple together over common pursuits and gives them a reservoir of strength to draw upon during challenging times. The shared pursuit of spiritual goals can be particularly bonding, as these goals often relate to the deepest questions of life, fostering a partnership that is both intimate and expansive.

Spirituality can turn relationships into sanctuaries, where individuals feel completely safe and nourished. Spiritual practices like prayer, meditation, or ritual can create a sacred space within the relationship, where partners can retreat from the stresses of the external world. In this spiritual refuge, individuals can share vulnerabilities and heal together, strengthening their bond and deepening their intimacy. This sanctuary becomes a foundational pillar of the relationship, where partners can find peace and restoration, no matter what life throws their way.

Engaging with spirituality can broaden perspectives, allowing individuals to see beyond the minutiae of daily life and understand the greater cosmic play at work. This broader perspective can alleviate stresses related to material concerns and interpersonal conflicts, as individuals learn to view their relationship within a larger existential context. Such a perspective encourages partners to value the present moment with one another and to cherish their connection as a precious conduit to the divine or as a significant component of their life's journey.

While spirituality offers numerous benefits to intimate relationships, it is not without its challenges. Discrepancies in spiritual beliefs or practices can create rifts if not approached openly and respectfully. Additionally, an overemphasis on spiritual compatibility can sometimes overshadow other important relational foundations such as emotional connection and physical compatibility. Therefore, while spirituality can profoundly enhance intimacy, it should be integrated thoughtfully and respectfully, with an openness to each partner's evolving spiritual expressions.

In conclusion, spirituality can significantly enhance intimate relationships by deepening communication, improving conflict resolution, fostering mutual growth, creating shared meaning, providing a sanctuary, and broadening perspectives. These enhancements not only strengthen the relationship but also enrich the individual lives of the partners involved. As couples navigate the complexities of their journeys together, integrating spirituality into their relational framework can offer a rich, supportive, and transformative dimension to their partnership, making it more resilient and more fulfilling in the deepest sense.

CHAPTER III

Unlocking Mystical Powers Within

Harnessing Energy Through Tantra

Tantra is known as an ancient spiritual tradition that originated in India, deeply rooted in the mystical philosophies of Hinduism and Buddhism. It transcends conventional understanding of sexuality and spirituality by intertwining these realms, proposing that physical acts, especially but not exclusively sexual, can be pathways to spiritual enlightenment. This section explores how Tantra harnesses energy for spiritual, emotional, and physical enhancement, its philosophical underpinnings, practices involved, and the broader implications of its teachings.

At its core, Tantra is based on the belief that the material world is not opposed to the spiritual world but is a reflection of it. The physical body is seen as a sacred temple that houses the divine spirit. The main goal of Tantra is to harness the energies contained within our bodies—often sexual energy—as a vehicle for spiritual ascension and enlightenment. This philosophy contends that all human experiences, particularly those involving pleasure or desire, can be paths to spiritual growth if approached with the right intention and awareness.

Tantra challenges the more ascetic traditions, which seek spiritual purity through the renunciation of worldly pleasures. Instead, it embraces these elements, integrating them into spiritual practice. This integration is predicated on the principle of non-duality (Advaita), which suggests that enlightenment does not necessitate escaping from the world but rather seeing the divine in all aspects of it.

Tantric practices are varied but share common goals: to weave together the many strands of life (the literal meaning of 'tantra') and channel what might otherwise be scattered energies into a coherent, divine encounter. These practices can be broadly categorized into rituals, meditations, and yogas.

Tantric rituals often involve mantras (chanting), yantras (symbolic diagrams), and mudras (symbolic gestures) that are believed to concentrate and channel spiritual energies. Sexual rituals, which are the most well-known aspect of Tantra in the West, use the act of sex as a powerful tool to transcend the self. Partners engaging in these rituals view each other as manifestations of divine entities and through their union, aim to mirror the union of the divine feminine and masculine, thus experiencing a profound spiritual wholeness and enlightenment.

Tantric meditation includes practices that involve visualizing deities and internal energies and sometimes the intricate channeling of these energies through the body's chakras (energy centers). These meditations are often designed to awaken the Kundalini, a dormant energy said to reside at the base of the spine. When successfully awakened and guided through the chakras, Kundalini can lead to higher states of consciousness and spiritual realization.

Unlike the more familiar Hatha Yoga, which primarily involves physical postures, Tantric yoga focuses on various physical and mental exercises that prepare the body and mind for spiritual experiences. These practices include but are not limited to breath control techniques (pranayama), the engagement of bodily locks (bandhas), and the use of sounds (nada yoga), all intended to harness and manipulate spiritual energy.

The fundamental aspect of Tantra is its focus on energy: cultivating it, harnessing it, and channeling it for spiritual, emotional, and physical well-being. This energy is not merely a metaphorical concept but is considered a tangible entity that can be felt, manipulated, and transformed through disciplined practice. The process of harnessing this energy is not linear; it requires continuous effort, guidance from experienced practitioners, and a profound commitment to the Tantric path.

The most striking feature of how Tantra harnesses energy is through its inclusive approach. It recognizes the potential in everyday experiences and bodily functions as means to spiritual elevation. This inclusivity breaks down the barriers between the sacred and the profane, offering a holistic spiritual path that is accessible to everyone, regardless of their stage of life or spiritual development.

The implications of Tantric practices are extensive. On a personal level, individuals who practice Tantra often report enhanced emotional resilience, more profound relationships, and a deepened sense of peace and contentment. Physically, Tantric practices can improve bodily health and sexual vitality, which are often seen as side benefits of the spiritual work.

On a broader scale, Tantra's philosophy and practices offer a radical critique of societal norms regarding sexuality and spirituality. By sanctifying the body and its desires, Tantra challenges prevailing religious and cultural attitudes that view the physical and the spiritual as separate or even opposed realms. This critique can foster a more holistic understanding of human nature, one that integrates rather than segregates different aspects of life.

In conclusion, Tantra represents a comprehensive spiritual path that uses a variety of practices to harness energy, particularly sexual energy, as a means to spiritual enlightenment. Its non-dualistic philosophy encourages a holistic integration of the spiritual and the physical, offering transformative potential for individual practitioners and societal norms about spirituality and sexuality. As a dynamic and living tradition, Tantra continues to evolve, adapting to contemporary needs and contexts while remaining rooted in its ancient philosophies. This balance of adaptation and adherence makes Tantra particularly relevant in the modern world, providing tools for personal and collective transformation that are as pertinent today as they were centuries ago.

The Power of Rituals and Symbolism in Sexual Magic

Sexual magic, an esoteric discipline that intertwines the potent energies of sexuality with spiritual practices, harnesses rituals and symbolism to profound effect. By exploring the multifaceted roles of these elements, we can acquire a deeper understanding of how they are employed within various traditions to enhance spiritual connectivity and manifest desired outcomes. This section delves into the significance of rituals and symbolism in sexual magic, examining their historical roots, psychological impacts, and practical applications.

Rituals and symbols have been integral to religious and magical practices throughout history, serving as conduits for the sacred and the supernatural. In sexual magic, these elements are particularly potent, as they combine the intrinsic power of sexuality with metaphysical intentions. Historically, from the Tantric rituals of Hinduism and Buddhism to the secretive practices of Western occult traditions, sexuality has been a symbol of life's creative force. In these contexts, rituals involving sexual acts are often meticulously designed to channel this immense energy towards spiritual enlightenment or magical realization.

In ancient Tantric texts, for instance, sexual union (Maithuna) is not merely physical but a ritualistic performance involving specific gestures, words, and symbols that collectively aim to transcend the individual self and realize a state of divine unity. Similarly, in Western traditions influenced by figures like Aleister Crowley, sexual magical rituals often involve elaborate symbolic frameworks that include ceremonial tools, invocations, and carefully structured acts designed to manipulate spiritual energies.

The power of symbolism in sexual magic cannot be overstated. Symbols serve as the language through which the unconscious can communicate with the conscious mind, bridging the gap between the seen and the unseen. In the context of sexual magic, common symbols include the lingam and the yoni, which represent the male and female sexual organs, respectively. These are not merely physical representations but are imbued with rich spiritual significance, symbolizing the union of divine masculine and feminine energies—the active and receptive forces of the universe.

Other symbols frequently used in sexual magic include the chalice and the blade, which also represent the feminine and masculine principles. When used in ritual contexts, these objects become metaphysical tools that facilitate the transmutation of sexual energy into spiritual power. The integration of these symbols into sexual magic rituals helps practitioners focus their intentions, amplify their desires, and reinforce the spiritual underpinnings of their practices.

Rituals in sexual magic are complex ceremonies that structure the chaotic potential of sexual energy. These rituals typically follow a sequence that includes purification, invocation, the act of union (physical or symbolic), and finally, the direction of the generated energy towards a specific purpose. The purification process, often involving baths, fasting, or other cleansing practices, prepares the participants physically and spiritually. Invocation calls upon divine energies or deities to preside over and bless the act. The union, whether actual sexual intercourse or a symbolic act involving ceremonial tools (such as inserting the blade into the chalice), is the climax of the ritual, generating a surge of energy that is believed to be potent enough to influence spiritual and physical realities.

The meticulous nature of these rituals serves multiple functions. First, it creates a sacred space that distinguishes the ordinary from the magical, setting the stage for a transformation of consciousness. Second, the ritual act focuses the participants' wills, aligning personal desires with universal energies. Third, it provides a safe and structured environment in which to explore the potent forces of sexuality in a spiritually constructive manner.

The use of rituals and symbolism in sexual magic also has profound psychological impacts. Carl Jung's theory of archetypes suggests that symbols resonate with the collective unconscious, evoking deep emotional responses. In sexual magic, the symbols and ritualistic acts tap into these archetypal images, facilitating deeper psychological integration and personal transformation. For instance, the ritual enactment of divine union can help individuals reconcile their own masculine and feminine aspects, leading to a more balanced and integrated personality.

Moreover, the ritual structure provides psychological reassurance, lending a sense of control and safety as individuals navigate the often turbulent waters of their psyche. This is particularly important in sexual magic, where the primal forces of sexuality can be overwhelming. Rituals help contain and direct these forces, providing a framework within which they can be experienced and utilized safely and effectively.

In practical terms, the rituals and symbols of sexual magic are used for various purposes, including spiritual enlightenment, healing, and the manifestation of specific goals. Practitioners often report enhanced feelings of connection with their partners, deepened self-awareness, and a renewed sense of purpose. The directed energy resulting from sexual magical practices can also be used to influence other areas of life, such as creativity, career, and personal growth endeavors.

In conclusion, the power of rituals and symbolism in sexual magic is a key component of its practice and effectiveness. These elements not only facilitate the safe and focused use of sexual energy but also enrich the spiritual experience by connecting the practitioner to deeper universal truths through symbolic language. As both a spiritual path and a method of personal transformation, sexual magic offers a unique confluence of the physical and the spiritual, mediated by the profound symbolic and ritualistic practices that define it. As modern practitioners continue to explore and adapt these ancient practices, the potential for growth and transformation through sexual magic remains vast and deeply significant.

Meditation and Visualization Techniques for Spiritual Connection

In the quest for spiritual connection, meditation and visualization emerge as powerful tools that transcend mere relaxation to delve into the profound realms of self-discovery and communion with the universe. This section explores these techniques, elucidating how they serve as conduits to spiritual enrichment and detailing their application for deeper self-awareness and connectivity.

Meditation, a practice that is rooted in ancient traditions, is the art of focusing and quieting the mind to achieve inner peace and spiritual insight. Its benefits are not solely confined to spiritual elevation but extend to emotional and physical health, enhancing mindfulness and stress reduction. The process involves several steps, beginning with choosing a quiet environment free from distractions. This setting fosters an atmosphere conducive to introspection and focus. Practitioners are advised to adopt a comfortable posture, such as sitting cross-legged, lying down, or even walking slowly in a serene area. The key is bodily comfort without sedation, to maintain alertness throughout the session.

Breathing techniques are integral to meditation. The practitioner focuses on slow, deep breaths to steady the mind and cultivate an awareness of the present moment. This focus on breath acts as an anchor, minimizing distractions and promoting a state of calmness. Over time, this practice helps detach from the cacophony of daily life and enter a tranquil, contemplative state where spiritual connections can be forged.

Visualization, or guided imagery, is a complementary practice that involves conjuring mental images that evoke feelings of peace, connectedness, and spiritual awakening. Unlike meditation, which often focuses on clearing the mind, visualization is active and dynamic. It uses the imagination to visit mental landscapes that are imbued with symbolic significance. For instance, visualizing a tranquil forest or a serene beach can transport the practitioner to places that resonate with their spiritual quests.

The power of visualization lies in its ability to harness the subconscious mind. Individuals can foster a deeper connection with these elements by imagining vivid scenarios aligned with personal spiritual symbols—such as light, water, or specific deities—and facilitate a transcendent experience. This practice enhances emotional depth and bolsters the spiritual journey by embedding these experiences within the psyche.

Combining meditation and visualization can amplify their benefits. A typical session might begin with meditation to stabilize the mind and body, followed by a transition to visualization techniques. For instance, after reaching a meditative state, a practitioner might visualize a light emanating from their heart, expanding to encompass the room, the home, and eventually the universe. This imagery of expanding light can symbolize the dissolution of personal boundaries and a merging with the universal essence.

Maintaining regular practice is crucial for those embarking on this spiritual journey. Consistency deepens the connection established through meditation and visualization, making the spiritual experience more profound and accessible. Moreover, the journey of spiritual connection is highly personal and subjective, often shaped by individual beliefs and experiences. Therefore, practitioners should feel empowered to adapt techniques to their unique spiritual needs and contexts.

Additionally, journaling after sessions can enhance understanding and retention of the spiritual insights gained. Writing down experiences can clarify thoughts and feelings that arose during meditation and visualization, providing a reflective space to understand and integrate these revelations.

Spiritual mentors or communities can also be pivotal in guiding individuals through their journey. These resources can provide personalized advice, support, and motivation, which are invaluable for navigating the complexities of spiritual practices. Engaging with a community offers the added benefit of shared experiences and collective wisdom, enriching the individual's practice.

In conclusion, meditation and visualization are profound tools for cultivating spiritual connections. They provide a pathway to personal tranquility and emotional balance and a deeper, more meaningful engagement with the spiritual dimensions of life. By incorporating these practices into everyday routines, individuals can navigate the depths of their being and experience a closer union with the universal energies that pervade our world. The journey towards spiritual connection is intricate and deeply personal, yet enriched immeasurably by these ancient and transformative techniques. Through dedicated practice, reflective journaling, and community engagement, one can navigate this path with insight and grace, achieving a harmonious balance between the self and the vast cosmos around us.

Awakening Kundalini Energy for Spiritual Growth

In the diverse tapestry of spiritual practices, the awakening of Kundalini energy is a profound and often mystical journey aimed at achieving spiritual enlightenment and transformation. This section delves into the concept of Kundalini, exploring how practitioners can stimulate this dormant energy for personal and spiritual growth.

Kundalini is conceptualized in Hindu philosophy as a form of divine feminine energy (or Shakti) located at the base of the spine. Traditionally depicted as a coiled serpent, Kundalini lies dormant until awakened, at this point, it ascends through the chakras—energy centers in the body—reaching up to the crown chakra at the top of the head. This journey through the chakras is believed to unlock a profound spiritual enlightenment and a deep internal purification, aligning the physical, emotional, and spiritual dimensions.

The process of awakening Kundalini is intricate and requires precise practice, often guided by a knowledgeable mentor, known as a guru. The most common practice associated with this awakening is Kundalini Yoga, which combines postures (asanas), specific breathing techniques (pranayama), meditation, and chanting mantras. Each element of Kundalini Yoga activates the body's energy systems, prepares the chakras for the ascent of Kundalini, and safeguards the practitioner's mind and body during this intense process.

Kundalini Yoga begins with asanas that stimulate energy flow from the lower chakras up to the higher chakras. These postures are designed to increase flexibility, strengthen the body, and open the channels through which Kundalini will travel. The importance of a strong physical foundation cannot be overstated, as the energy released during the awakening process can be overwhelming and, if not properly managed, potentially disruptive.

Breathing techniques in Kundalini Yoga mainly focus on enhancing the flow of prana, or life force, throughout the body. Techniques such as the "Breath of Fire" (rapid, rhythmic breathing through the nostrils) are used to heat the body and awaken the lower chakras, thereby facilitating the rise of Kundalini. These breathing practices are critical in maintaining the balance of energies and supporting the sustained concentration needed for meditation.

Meditation in Kundalini Yoga involves visualizing the energy rising from the spine's base through each chakra, culminating at the crown chakra. This visualization not only aids in the mental journey of energy ascent but also helps the practitioner handle the spiritual revelations and psychic experiences that often accompany this awakening. Using mantras or sacred sounds further empowers the meditation, aligning the practitioner's vibrations with those of the universe.

The role of a guru or a trained instructor is indispensable in the practice of awakening Kundalini. This mentor ensures that the techniques are performed correctly and that the practitioner is both spiritually and physically prepared for the experiences that may arise. The guru also provides the necessary support to navigate the profound and sometimes turbulent changes that accompany the release of Kundalini.

While the physical and mental benefits of Kundalini Yoga are significant—ranging from improved mental clarity and increased physical strength to profound inner peace—the ultimate goal is spiritual. Practitioners report experiences of expansive spiritual connection, a sense of universal love, and insights into their purpose and the nature of reality. These experiences can be transformative, profoundly altering life perspectives and behaviors.

However, the path of Kundalini awakening is not without challenges. It demands dedication, discipline, and a readiness to face one's own subconscious barriers. The energy released can sometimes manifest in intense physical, emotional, or psychological symptoms, commonly called Kundalini Syndrome. These manifestations might include mood swings, sensory over-sensitivity, or even altered states of consciousness. Such potentialities underscore the importance of practicing under the supervision of a competent teacher.

In addition to Kundalini Yoga, other spiritual practices such as meditation retreats, chanting, and deep prayer can also facilitate the awakening process. These practices help purify the mind and body, creating a fertile ground for spiritual growth. Dietary considerations also play a role, with many practitioners adopting a clean, vegetarian diet to reduce bodily toxins and enhance vibrational levels.

The journey of awakening Kundalini is ultimately a deeply personal experience, unique to each practitioner. It offers a path to profound spiritual depth and an expanded state of consciousness, connecting the individual with the universal energies that govern existence. Those who embark on this path often find it transformative, catalyzing personal evolution and a renewed sense of purpose.

In conclusion, the awakening of Kundalini energy is a sacred process that offers significant spiritual benefits. It integrates physical postures, breathing techniques, and meditation to stimulate and guide the release of this potent energy through the chakras. Individuals can achieve remarkable spiritual insights and growth through proper guidance, commitment, and mindful practice. This mystical journey enhances personal well-being and contributes to the collective elevation of human consciousness. As such, Kundalini Yoga remains a vital practice for those seeking to explore the deeper realms of spirituality and connect with the divine energies of the universe.

CHAPTER IV

Healing and Transformation Through Sexual Magic

Healing Trauma and Blockages Through Sacred Sexuality

Sacred sexuality offers a transformative path for healing trauma and clearing emotional and energetic blockages that impede personal and spiritual growth. This section explores the principles of sacred sexuality, its roots in ancient wisdom, and its applications in modern therapeutic contexts, providing a comprehensive look at its role in healing and transformation.

Sacred sexuality, often associated with Eastern traditions like Tantra and Taoism, views sexual energy as a powerful force for physical healing and spiritual enlightenment. Unlike the more conventional views of sexuality focused on physical pleasure or procreation, sacred sexuality approaches sexual energy as a sacred and life-affirming force that can be harnessed for deep healing and personal evolution. This perspective sees sexual union as not just a physical act but as a profound spiritual and emotional connection that can transcend ordinary experiences of intimacy.

The concept of healing trauma through sacred sexuality is premised on the belief that sexual energy can unlock and release blockages deeply embedded within the body and psyche. Trauma, whether from emotional, physical, or sexual abuse, can create substantial disruptions in an individual's energetic body, leading to issues like anxiety, depression, or emotional detachment. Sacred sexuality practices aim to gently and safely release these blockages, restoring balance and facilitating a reconnection with one's self and others.

Practitioners of sacred sexuality use various techniques to achieve healing. These include but are not limited to, controlled breathing, meditation, energy work, and intentional, mindful sexual union. Breathing and meditation are foundational practices that help individuals centre themselves, cultivate presence, and prepare their bodies and mind for the energy work to come. These practices also help to reduce the psychological resistance often encountered in trauma recovery.

Energy work in sacred sexuality often involves manipulating the chakras or energy centers within the body. Practitioners believe that trauma can cause these chakras to become blocked or misaligned. Techniques such as chakra meditation, visualization, and even hands-on energy healing are used to address these disruptions. The goal is to encourage the flow of sexual energy throughout the body, thereby initiating healing and the reclamation of bodily autonomy and power.

The practice of mindful sexual union, perhaps the most profound aspect of sacred sexuality, requires deep trust and communication between partners. This process is not about achieving sexual gratification but about using sexual energy as a medium for emotional and spiritual nurturing. During these sacred encounters, partners are encouraged to maintain a focus on their internal experiences rather than merely the physical sensations, allowing for a transfer and release of traumatic energies.

Guidance from experienced practitioners is critical in sacred sexuality, especially for individuals healing from trauma. The therapeutic setting must be one of absolute safety and confidentiality, where individuals can explore these vulnerabilities without fear of judgment or re-traumatization. Qualified therapists who specialize in sacred sexuality are adept at creating a supportive environment that facilitates this kind of deep, transformational work.

The integration of sacred sexuality into trauma therapy can offer a pathway to reclaiming power and agency that trauma survivors often feel they have lost. It provides a space for survivors to rewrite their narratives around sexuality and intimacy, transforming their experiences from sources of pain to sources of strength and renewal. Furthermore, it can promote a greater sense of connection to others and the universe, aspects often diminished by traumatic experiences.

Critics of sacred sexuality argue that its practices can be misused, potentially exacerbating the trauma if not handled with utmost care and professionalism. Therefore, the importance of working with well-trained and ethically responsible practitioners cannot be overstressed. It is also crucial for individuals to proceed at their own pace, gradually building trust and comfort with the practices and the practitioner.

In modern therapeutic practice, elements of sacred sexuality are increasingly being integrated with psychotherapeutic techniques to provide a holistic approach to trauma recovery. This integration acknowledges the complex nature of trauma, which affects the body, mind, and spirit. Therapies that encompass only verbal or cognitive approaches may leave the somatic and energetic impacts of trauma unaddressed. Sacred sexuality can fill this gap with its comprehensive view of the human experience.

Moreover, the principles of sacred sexuality also resonate in self-help and self-care practices, where individuals use techniques like meditation, breathwork, and energy work to foster personal growth and well-being independently. These practices can be particularly empowering for trauma survivors, providing them with tools to manage their healing process actively.

In conclusion, sacred sexuality offers a nuanced and profoundly transformative approach to healing trauma and emotional blockages. By re-envisioning the role of sexual energy as a vehicle for spiritual and emotional well-being, it challenges conventional narratives about sexuality and trauma recovery. With the right guidance and a respectful, mindful approach, sacred sexuality can lead to significant personal transformation and profound healing, ultimately enabling individuals to lead fuller, more connected lives. As this field continues to evolve, it holds the promise of further innovations in healing practices, contributing to broader societal shifts in understanding and addressing trauma.

Overcoming Shame and Guilt Surrounding Sexuality

In the landscape of human emotions, shame and guilt are profound influencers, particularly when they relate to sexuality. These emotions can significantly impact individual well-being and the capacity for healthy relational dynamics. This section explores the origins of sexual shame and guilt, their effects on individuals, and practical approaches for overcoming these debilitating emotions to foster a healthier sexual identity.

Sexual shame and guilt often stem from cultural, religious, and familial teachings that frame sexuality as inherently problematic or sinful outside specific contexts. These messages can be internalized from a young age, leading to deep-seated feelings of shame and guilt that manifest in various aspects of life, including intimacy and personal relationships. The pervasive nature of these emotions can cause individuals to disconnect from their sexual selves, leading to an array of psychological and emotional issues, such as anxiety, depression, and low self-esteem.

Understanding the origins of these feelings is the first step in overcoming them. In many societies, historical and religious ideologies have dictated strict codes of conduct regarding sexual behaviour, often disproportionately targeting feminine sexuality but impacting all genders. These norms can lead individuals to feel that their natural desires are inappropriate or immoral, causing feelings of shame when they cannot conform to expected standards. Furthermore, experiences of sexual judgment or trauma can exacerbate these feelings, embedding them more deeply into the psyche.

The consequences of untreated sexual shame and guilt are far-reaching. At an individual level, they can stunt the development of a healthy sexual identity and lead to problems such as sexual dysfunction, relationship difficulties, and aversion to intimacy. Socially, these feelings can contribute to a culture of secrecy and repression, affecting how sexuality is discussed and perceived in the broader community.

Overcoming these emotions involves a multifaceted approach that includes education, therapy, and community support. Education plays a critical role in dispelling myths and misconceptions about sexuality. Comprehensive sex education that promotes sex positivity and an understanding of sexual health can help dismantle the foundations of sexual shame. This education should begin early and be inclusive of all sexual orientations and identities, emphasizing the normalcy of sexual desire and the importance of consent and communication.

Therapy can also be beneficial, particularly approaches that focus on emotional processing and cognitive restructuring. Cognitive-behavioral therapy (or CBT) and other forms of psychotherapy can help individuals identify and challenge the irrational beliefs that fuel their feelings of shame and guilt. Through therapy, individuals can learn to reframe their thoughts about sexuality in a more positive and accepting light.

Moreover, experiential therapies such as drama therapy or art therapy permit for the creative expression of sexual narratives, offering a release from the shame built up around these stories. These therapeutic approaches provide safe spaces to explore and reconcile feelings of shame and guilt, which are essential for healing.

Community support is equally vital. Finding and engaging with sex-positive communities can validate an individual's experiences and feelings, reducing the sense of isolation that shame and guilt often bring. These communities can be found in various forms, such as support groups, online forums, or local organizations dedicated to sexual well-being. In these spaces, shared experiences can foster a sense of belonging and support, crucial for emotional recovery and growth.

Personal practices such as mindfulness and meditation can also aid in overcoming sexual shame and guilt. These practices help individuals develop a greater awareness of their thoughts as well as feelings, recognize patterns of self-judgment, and cultivate self-compassion. Being present and compassionate with oneself makes it possible to detach and heal from these negative emotions slowly.

The journey to overcome sexual shame and guilt is deeply personal and often challenging, involving confronting painful emotions and entrenched beliefs. However, the freedom gained from releasing these burdens can profoundly affect one's quality of life and relationships. As individuals work through their feelings of shame and guilt, they often discover a newfound capacity for joy, intimacy, and fulfillment in their sexual lives.

In conclusion, while the path to overcoming sexual shame and guilt is complex and layered, it is also gratifying. It requires a holistic approach involving personal introspection, education, professional help, and community support. Society plays a role, too; as cultural and social narratives about sexuality become more open and affirming, less individual shame will be a common part of the sexual experience. Ultimately, addressing these issues benefits individuals and contributes to the health and maturity of society as a whole, promoting a more compassionate and understanding approach to human sexuality. This healing journey not only liberates one from the shackles of past indoctrinations but also paves the way for a healthier, more integrated sexual identity.

Using Sexual Energy for Personal and Spiritual Growth

Sexual energy is one of the most potent and vital forces in human existence, not only for procreation but also as a vehicle for personal and spiritual growth. This section explores how sexual energy can be harnessed for enhancing individual development and deepening spiritual connections, integrating perspectives from various traditions and practices that highlight the transformative power of this primal force.

Sexual energy, referred to as Kundalini in Hindu traditions and Chi or Qi in Taoist practice, is believed to be a key to unlocking profound spiritual enlightenment and physical well-being. It is this energy, when properly directed, that can promote healing, creativity, and a deeper sense of connectivity with the universe. The foundation of using sexual energy for growth lies in understanding its nature not merely as a biological drive but as a significant element of our spiritual and energetic makeup.

Central to this perspective is the concept of the chakras, seven energy centers located throughout the body, each corresponding to different aspects of our physical and emotional life. In traditional teachings, the sexual energy residing in the sacral chakra can be activated and guided through these centers, facilitating a transformative energy flow that enhances each chakra's attributes. This process, often called the rising of Kundalini, seeks to balance and purify the individual's energy system, promoting health, emotional clarity, and spiritual awakening.

Harnessing sexual energy for personal growth involves practices that cultivate sexual vitality and direct it towards personal development goals. Techniques such as meditation, breathwork, and mindfulness are commonly employed to increase awareness and control over this energy. Meditation techniques, for example, can focus on the visualization of energy moving through the body, helping to clear blockages in the chakras and build a stronger, more harmonious energy flow. Breathwork also plays a crucial role, with specific breathing patterns used to raise or stabilize energy levels, aiding in the control and elevation of Kundalini.

In the realm of spirituality, sexual energy is used not only for personal healing but also to gain a more profound connection with the divine. Many mystical traditions use sexual symbolism and rituals to represent the union of the divine masculine and the feminine, an allegory for the inner harmony and spiritual wholeness one might achieve. This spiritual aspect of sexual energy is also emphasized in the practice of sacred sexuality, where sexual acts are revered as not only a physical union but also a spiritual act that mirrors cosmic processes.

The Taoist practices provide a vivid blueprint for using sexual energy in a way that prioritizes spiritual ascension and health. Techniques which include Qi Gong and Tai Chi focus on the cultivation, balance, and flow of Chi throughout the body, with specific practices tailored to harnessing sexual Chi to invigorate the body's energy system. This perspective is not about repression but about the transformation of sexual energy into a tool for achieving greater vitality and spiritual insight.

Moreover, modern interpretations of using sexual energy suggest that it can drive creativity and enhance productivity. Artists, writers, and thinkers often speak of the generative nature of sexual energy when channelled into creative endeavours. This idea is mirrored in the concept of sublimation in psychology, where sexual impulses are redirected into socially and personally enriching activities, leading to higher psychological development.

However, managing sexual energy wisely requires discipline and awareness. Uncontrolled or misdirected sexual energy can lead to compulsive behaviors, while repressed energy can stagnate, leading to emotional numbness or depression. Therefore, education about sexual health and energy management is crucial. Learning to handle sexual desires responsibly and understanding their place in personal and spiritual development can help individuals make knowledgeable decisions about their sexual health and spiritual practices.

One effective approach for cultivating and managing sexual energy is through yoga, particularly Kundalini Yoga, which includes a numbers of postures, breathing exercises, and meditations specifically designed to awaken and channel Kundalini energy. These practices help in refining one's sensitivity to energy fluctuations and developing the ability to modulate them consciously.

In therapeutic settings, sexual energy is increasingly recognized for its healing potential. Therapists who specialize in sexual health might integrate discussions and practices related to sexual energy into their sessions, helping clients address and heal from sexual dysfunctions, trauma, and emotional blockages. The integration of sexual energy concepts into therapy can empower clients, helping them to reclaim their energy and use it for healing and personal transformation.

In conclusion, sexual energy is a powerful catalyst for personal and spiritual growth. Its proper management can lead to profound personal changes, including enhanced physical health, emotional healing, and spiritual enlightenment. The practices discussed facilitate a deeper understanding of one's energy system and promote a harmonious balance between physical desires and spiritual aspirations. By embracing the holistic power of sexual energy, individuals can explore new dimensions of their being and experience a more integrated existence. As society progresses in understanding and accepting this energy, the potential for collective and individual transformation expands, paving the way for a more conscious and enlightened engagement with the fundamental aspects of life.

Case Studies and Success Stories

Sexual magic, a term steeped in the mystique of both ancient lore and modern esoteric practices, refers to the use of sexual energy and rituals to manifest desires, attract positive changes, and enhance personal empowerment. This section explores various case studies and success stories that highlight the efficacy of sexual magic in personal transformation and spiritual enlightenment.

Sexual magic is rooted in the belief that sexual energy is one of the most powerful forces available to humans for spiritual and mundane purposes. This concept is found in numerous traditions, including Western esoteric traditions like Thelema and Kabbalah, as well as Eastern practices such as Tantra. These traditions teach that by harnessing and directing sexual energy through ritual and intention, individuals can effect significant changes in their lives and the world around them.

Case Study 1: Healing and Reconciliation

One notable case involved a couple, referred to here as John and Mary, who were experiencing marital difficulties characterized by communication breakdowns and emotional disconnect. They participated in a series of sexual magic workshops that focused on healing and reconnecting. Through rituals that emphasized intentional touch, synchronized breathing, and visualizations of energy exchange, they reported a renewed sense of connection and understanding. The practice helped them to break down barriers of resentment and miscommunication, allowing them to rebuild their relationship on a bedrock of renewed trust and intimacy.

Case Study 2: Career Advancement

Another case involved an individual named Lisa, a professional struggling with career advancement. Feeling stuck in her current role with little opportunity for promotion, Lisa turned to sexual magic to focus her intentions and manifest career opportunities. By incorporating sexual rituals into her visualization practices—specifically focusing on embodying qualities of leadership and confidence—she claimed to have experienced a significant shift in her professional demeanor. This change was soon recognized by her superiors, leading to a promotion and opportunities to lead major projects.

Case Study 3: Creative Breakthroughs

Thomas, a writer suffering from severe writer's block, found sexual magic rituals to be a breakthrough method for restoring his creativity. He engaged in practices that involved channeling sexual energy into his creative process, using specific symbols and mantras during rituals to enhance his imaginative powers. Over the course of several months, Thomas not only overcame his writer's block but also completed his novel, which was later successfully published. He credited sexual magic for his renewed creativity and the completion of his work.

Case Study 4: Personal Empowerment and Self-Esteem

A young woman named Emma used sexual magic to overcome deep-seated issues of self-esteem and body image. Through rituals that celebrated her body as a vessel of divine energy and practiced in a supportive group setting, Emma learned to view herself as powerful and deserving of respect. This newfound confidence had a domino effect in her life, improving her interpersonal relationships and professional interactions.

Case Study 5: Overcoming Financial Hardship

Mark, facing significant financial distress, turned to sexual magic as a last resort to improve his financial situation. By focusing his sexual energy during rituals specifically designed to attract abundance and prosperity, Mark reported unexpected opportunities for freelance work that helped alleviate his immediate financial troubles. He attributed these opportunities to the clarity and intent fostered by his sexual magic practices.

These case studies illustrate the potential of sexual magic not only to address specific personal and professional issues but also to promote broader spiritual and psychological growth. Participants in these case studies often report a profound sense of empowerment and connectivity with a higher purpose, which they attribute to their engagement with sexual magic.

The success of sexual magic, as demonstrated in these cases, underscores the importance of intentionality, belief, and the responsible use of energy in the practice. It is not merely the sexual acts themselves but the conscious intent and ritualistic framework that direct the energy toward desired outcomes. Practitioners emphasize the necessity of clear goals, ethical considerations, and often, the guidance of an experienced mentor to navigate the complexities of these practices safely and effectively.

Moreover, these success stories contribute to a larger discourse on the potential for alternative spiritual practices to effect real change in people's lives. They challenge the stigma often associated with esoteric practices by highlighting their practical benefits and transformative potential.

In conclusion, sexual magic represents a potent tool for personal transformation and the manifestation of one's desires. The case studies discussed provide a glimpse into these practices' diverse applications and profound impact on individuals' personal, professional, and spiritual lives. As more people seek holistic and integrative approaches to personal growth and healing, sexual magic is likely to gain further attention and legitimacy as a meaningful and effective spiritual practice. These narratives both serve to demystify the practice and illuminate the profound connection between sexuality and spirituality, offering a compelling perspective on the power of human energy and intention.

CHAPTER V

Deepening Connection Through Rituals and Practices

Rituals for Enhancing Intimacy and Connection

In the modern age, where digital interactions often replace face-to-face connections, the art of cultivating deep, meaningful relationships can sometimes seem like a lost practice. Yet, the human craving for intimacy and connection remains as strong as ever, driving individuals to seek pathways that foster genuine bonds. This section explores various rituals that can enhance intimacy and connection, drawing on traditions worldwide and insights from contemporary relationship science.

At its core, intimacy is about closeness, understanding, and trust. It transcends physical boundaries, encompassing emotional, intellectual, and spiritual connections. With their inherent ability to create shared meaning and experiences, rituals offer powerful tools for deepening these connections. They can range from simple daily practices to more elaborate ceremonies, all aimed at reinforcing the bonds between individuals.

One foundational ritual for enhancing intimacy is active listening. This entails fully concentrating on what is being said rather than passively hearing the speaker's message. Active listening rituals might include setting aside a specific time each day to share thoughts and feelings without interruptions or distractions. This dedicated time encourages openness and vulnerability, essential ingredients for intimacy. It signals to partners that their experiences and emotions are valued and respected, laying the groundwork for deeper understanding and empathy.

Another powerful ritual is the expression of gratitude. Research has consistently shown that gratitude plays a significant role in strengthening relationships. Couples can incorporate gratitude rituals into their daily routines, such as leaving appreciative notes for one another, sharing three things they are grateful for about each other at the end of the day, or creating a shared gratitude journal. These practices increase positive feelings towards each other and help buffer against the negative effects of conflict.

Physical touch, beyond sexual intimacy, holds profound power in conveying love, comfort, and connection. Simple rituals like holding hands during a walk, hugging for a full minute every day, or ensuring a kiss goodbye become a daily routine can significantly enhance feelings of closeness and security in a relationship. The physiological responses to physical touch—such as the release of oxytocin, often called as the "love hormone"—further cement the emotional bond between partners.

Creating rituals around shared experiences can also intensify intimacy. This might involve regular date nights but can also extend to less conventional practices, such as undertaking a new challenge together every month, whether it's learning a dance, cooking a complex meal, or hiking a trail. These shared adventures create unique memories and stories, reinforcing the couple's identity and fostering a sense of unity and teamwork.

Spiritual rituals, whether rooted in religious traditions or personal spiritual beliefs, can offer another dimension of connection. Practices such as meditating together, attending religious services, or even creating a personal ritual to honor the relationship can imbue it with a sense of sacredness and shared purpose. These rituals can help couples connect spiritually, exploring and deepening their shared values and visions for their lives together.

In addition to these personal rituals, community-based rituals can also significantly enhance intimacy and connection. Participating in community service, attending cultural or religious events together, or even creating a ritual to celebrate love and commitment in the presence of loved ones can reinforce the couple's bond and integrate their relationship within a broader social and cultural context.

The key to the success of these rituals lies in their regular practice and the intention behind them. Rituals should not be performed out of obligation but with a genuine desire to connect and grow closer. Flexibility is also essential; as relationships evolve, so too might the rituals that best serve them. Open communication about what feels meaningful and fulfilling is essential to ensuring that these practices continue to enhance intimacy and connection.

In conclusion, rituals offer a valuable toolkit for deepening intimacy and fostering relationship connections. By incorporating practices of active listening, expressing gratitude, engaging in physical touch, sharing experiences, and honoring spiritual connections, couples can create a rich tapestry of interactions that reinforce their bond. As society continues to navigate the challenges of modern connectivity, these timeless practices remind us of the power of intentional action in cultivating the deep, fulfilling relationships that are at the heart of the human experience. Through the thoughtful adoption and adaptation of rituals, individuals can enhance their intimate connections and contribute to a culture that values and nurtures genuine human connection.

Sacred Sexuality Practices for Couples

Sacred sexuality offers a transformative pathway for couples seeking not only deeper intimacy but also spiritual growth through their physical union. Rooted in ancient traditions that see sexual union as a profound conduit to higher consciousness, sacred sexuality practices can strengthen relationships by infusing them with greater emotional depth, mutual understanding, and a connection to the divine. This section explores the principles and practices of sacred sexuality that couples can adopt to enrich their relationships.

Sacred sexuality is an approach to intimacy that integrates the mind, body, and spirit, promoting a holistic connection between partners. Unlike the more common perceptions of sexuality, which often focus solely on physical pleasure, sacred sexuality considers the sexual union a sacred act that has the potential to open higher states of consciousness and healing. Several spiritual traditions, including Tantra from Hinduism and Buddhism, Taoist sexual practices, and the Western esoteric tradition influence this perspective.

At the core of sacred sexuality is the belief that sexual energy is a powerful life force that can be utilized for spiritual growth and healing. This energy, known as Kundalini in Tantra and Chi in Taoism, is thought to reside within the human body and can be awakened and channeled through sexual union. The practice involves more than just sexual intercourse; it includes a variety of physical and spiritual activities that help partners connect more deeply and move energy throughout their bodies in a transformative way.

Tantra, one of the most well-known systems of sacred sexuality, emphasizes the sanctity of all bodily functions and experiences, including sexuality. Tantric practices for couples often begin with setting a sacred space for intimacy. This might involve creating a comfortable and beautiful environment, using candles, incense, and soothing music to enhance the sensory experience. The goal is to step out of the mundane world and into a sacred space where couples can focus entirely on their connection.

Communication is also a vital component of Tantric practice. Partners are encouraged to engage in honest and open dialogue about their desires, boundaries, and spiritual intentions for their sexual union. This communication continues into their sexual practice, with check-ins to ensure both partners feel comfortable and connected throughout their experience.

Breathing exercises are used to sync the partners' energies before and during sexual activity. Techniques such as synchronized breathing or the "Breath of Fire" (rapid, rhythmic breathing through the nose) help to raise energy and increase intimacy. Eye contact, or "soul gazing," is another powerful tool used in Tantra to deepen connection. Partners maintain eye contact throughout their interaction to enhance emotional connectivity and nonverbal communication.

Taoism offers another rich tradition of sacred sexuality, focused on the harmonious balance of masculine and feminine energies within the body. Taoist practices often emphasize the conservation and transformation of sexual energy. Techniques such as the Microcosmic Orbit involve guiding sexual energy through the body's energy centers or chakras, enhancing vitality and spiritual awareness.

In addition, Taoist sexual practices include exercises for controlling and extending sexual energy, particularly for men, to avoid the loss of vital energies through ejaculation. Instead, sexual arousal is increased and circulated through the body to promote healing and rejuvenation. For women, practices might focus on harnessing sexual energy to open the heart and strengthen the emotional bond between partners.

Rituals play a crucial role in sacred sexuality, adding a layer of profundity and intention to sexual encounters. Couples might create rituals around their sexual encounters, such as bathing together before intimacy, offering massages, or practicing joint meditation focused on heart-opening or energy-raising mantras. These rituals help set intentions, align energies, and sanctify the physical union, making each encounter unique and meaningful.

For many couples, integrating sacred sexuality practices into daily life can be challenging but rewarding. It involves more than occasional practice; it requires a commitment to honor the sacredness of their connection continually. Daily practices might include non-sexual touch, words of affirmation, shared yoga or meditation sessions, and regular discussions about spiritual goals and emotional needs. These practices ensure that the sacredness of their connection permeates their everyday interactions, not just their sexual activities.

Couples who engage in sacred sexuality often report deeper emotional connections, enhanced communication, and a greater sense of presence within the relationship. Physically, they may experience improved sexual pleasure and intimacy. Spiritually, these practices can lead to a profound sense of unity and understanding, not only with each other but with the larger cosmos. This spiritual connectivity can be particularly healing for couples dealing with issues of trust, past traumas, or disconnect.

In conclusion, sacred sexuality offers couples a rich framework for exploring the depths of their physical, emotional, and spiritual connections. Through rituals, Tantric and Taoist practices, and integrating these principles into everyday life, couples can transform their relationships into profound partnerships that foster mutual growth and healing. These practices provide a pathway to not only enhanced intimacy but also personal and spiritual development, deepening the bonds of love through the sacred power of sexual union. By embracing these ancient wisdoms, couples can discover new relationship dimensions and experience the transformative power of sacred sexuality.

Exploring Sacred Union and Divine Partnership

The concepts of sacred union and divine partnership have gained considerable attention in contemporary discussions surrounding relationships and spirituality. These terms often describe relationships that transcend traditional romantic frameworks, offering a deeper, more spiritual connection between partners. This section delves into the essence of sacred unions and divine partnerships, exploring their characteristics, foundational principles, and the transformative impact they have on individuals and their collective growth.

Sacred union and divine partnership refer to a type of relationship where both individuals approach their connection with the intention of spiritual and personal development. Unlike conventional relationships that might focus primarily on mutual comfort and companionship, sacred unions are rooted in the growth- oriented dynamics of each partner. The relationship itself becomes a conduit for spiritual awakening and a mirror reflecting each partner's strengths and shadows.

The concept of a divine partnership involves the idea that relationships are predestined or divinely orchestrated. These partnerships are often characterized by a profound sense of recognition and familiarity as if the individuals have known each other beyond their current lifetime. This sense of eternity and destiny can profoundly influence how partners interact, perceive challenges, and support each other's spiritual paths.

A key characteristic of sacred unions is their emphasis on healing. Partners in such relationships often find that their connection brings up unresolved issues and emotional wounds to the surface. Rather than shy away from these challenges, sacred unions encourage individuals to confront and heal these aspects of themselves, using the relationship as a safe and supportive space. This process is reciprocal, with each partner acting as both healer and guide, fostering a journey of mutual evolution.

Another significant aspect of these relationships is the balance of masculine as well as feminine energies within the union, regardless of the partners' genders. Sacred unions strive for harmony between action and receptiveness, giving and receiving, strength and vulnerability. This energetic balance promotes a healthier, more holistic approach to both partners' lives and their relationship dynamics.

Divine partnerships are governed by principles that distinguish them from other types of relationships. One of the primary principles is unconditional love. This does not imply a relationship without boundaries or personal standards but rather a commitment to loving the partner without an agenda or condition. This love is about seeing and accepting the partner wholly, celebrating their essence beyond physical and emotional attributes.

Integrity and authenticity are also central to divine partnerships. These relationships thrive on transparency and honesty, where both individuals feel safe to express their true selves without fear of judgment or rejection. This authenticity allows partners to communicate openly, share their deepest fears, ambitions, and vulnerabilities, and support each other's true paths.

Spiritual alignment and purpose are also critical in divine partnerships. These couples often feel a shared mission or purpose that transcends individual goals, involving service to a community or a collective spiritual calling. This shared vision can strengthen their bond, providing a common ground for their energies and efforts.

Engaging in a sacred union or divine partnership can lead to profound personal transformation. Partners in such relationships often experience accelerated personal growth, as the relationship continuously prompts them to evolve and adapt. This transformation can be seen in areas such as self-awareness, emotional intelligence, and spiritual practices. Each partner becomes a catalyst for the other's development, challenging them to transcend their limitations and explore new spiritual depths.

Additionally, sacred unions can lead to greater life satisfaction and fulfillment. As partners navigate their journey together, they cultivate a deep sense of joy as well as contentment that comes from shared spiritual exploration and the realization of personal truths. The support and unconditional love present in divine partnerships reinforce a life of authenticity and freedom, encouraging each individual to live fully and passionately.

Sacred unions and divine partnerships are not without challenges despite their profound benefits. The intensity of such relationships can bring significant emotional upheaval. As partners reflect and amplify each other's subconscious issues, they might encounter periods of turmoil and conflict. Navigating these challenges requires maturity, commitment, and, most importantly, a willingness to engage in personal and joint healing processes.

Furthermore, maintaining balance between personal independence and the relationship's unity can be challenging. Each partner must honor their own path and individuality while nurturing the relationship's collective dimension. This balancing act is crucial for the sustainability of both partners' spiritual autonomy and the union's health.

Several practices can be beneficial for those in sacred unions or aspiring to such relationships. Regularly engaging in joint spiritual practices such as meditation, prayer, or ritual can enhance connection and alignment. Couples therapy or workshops focusing on spiritual relationships can provide tools and insights for managing the complexities of such deep connections. Lastly, community support from like-minded individuals or groups can offer external perspectives and encouragement.

In conclusion, sacred unions and divine partnerships represent a profound relational and spiritual fulfillment model. They challenge conventional notions of romance and partnership, emphasizing spiritual growth, healing, and unconditional love. While these relationships can be demanding, their potential to transform individuals and couples is immense. As society continues to explore and embrace these deep connections, we uncover new possibilities for love, partnership, and collective evolution in our increasingly interconnected world.

Integrating Spiritual Practices into Daily Life

Finding time and space for spirituality can be a challenge in the hustle and bustle of modern life. However, integrating spiritual practices into daily routines can provide profound benefits, including increased clarity, peace, and purpose. This section explores the importance of spiritual practices and offers guidance on seamlessly incorporating them into everyday life, enhancing both personal well-being and connectivity with the wider world.

Spiritual practices are activities that nurture spiritual growth as well as foster a deeper connection with the divine, however one chooses to define it. These practices can include meditation, prayer, reading spiritual texts, or engaging in rituals that align with one's spiritual beliefs. The benefits of such practices are well-documented and include enhanced emotional health, reduced stress levels, and improved overall happiness. Spiritually engaged individuals often report greater life satisfaction and a better capacity to cope with life's challenges.

Meditation and also mindfulness are among the most effective ways to integrate spirituality into daily life. Meditation involves sitting in quiet reflection for a period, focusing on the breath or a mantra to quiet the mind. This practice can start with as little as five minutes per day and gradually increase as one becomes more comfortable with the technique. Mindfulness extends this practice to everyday activities. It entails maintaining a moment-by-moment awareness of our feelings, thoughts, bodily sensations, as well as the surrounding environment.

Practicing mindfulness can transform mundane activities like eating, walking, or washing dishes into profound spiritual exercises, opening up a space for grace in the simplicity of everyday living.

For many, prayer is a foundational spiritual practice, providing a direct line to communicate with a higher power. It can be ritualistic or conversational and can occur at a set time of day or as needed. Integrating prayer into daily life can be as simple as starting the day with a morning prayer or blessing, using breaks or commutes to recite affirmations, or ending the day with a reflective prayer of gratitude. Affirmations are positive, personal, present-tense statements that foster a positive mental attitude and can be integrated into daily prayer to enhance spiritual and emotional well-being.

Reading and reflecting on spiritual texts is another method of integrating spiritual practice into daily life. This could involve reading a passage from a sacred scripture, spiritual book, or philosophical texts each morning or evening. The key is to reflect on the passage and find ways to apply its lessons throughout the day. This practice provides spiritual nourishment and deepens one's understanding and connection to their spiritual tradition.

Rituals can turn everyday routines into sacred moments. This might involve lighting a candle before meals, saying a blessing, or creating a personal ritual to start and end the workday. These small acts help sanctify daily life, making room for spirituality in the most ordinary days. Rituals can be particularly powerful in marking transitions, helping to segment the day and providing regular touchpoints for spiritual reflection.

Spending time in nature is a deeply spiritual practice for many people. It provides an opportunity to disconnect from the artificial and reconnect with the natural world. Integrating this practice can be as simple as taking a walk in a nearby park, maintaining a garden, or simply sitting under a tree during a lunch break. The rhythms of nature can help to realign one's own rhythms with the world around them, fostering a sense of peace and grounding.

Yoga combines physical postures, breathwork, and meditation, offering a comprehensive spiritual practice that nurtures body, mind, and spirit. Incorporating yoga or any form of conscious movement into daily routines can enhance physical health while providing spiritual benefits. Dedicating a small amount of time each day to this practice can significantly improve one's spiritual and physical well-being.

Spirituality does not have to be a solitary journey. Participating in a community of like-minded individuals can enhance one's spiritual practices. This might involve attending services at a place of worship, joining a meditation group, or participating in a study group focused on spiritual texts. Community involvement provides support and deepens one's practice through shared experiences and collective wisdom.

It is essential to approach the integration of spiritual practices with flexibility and patience. Not every practice will suit every individual, and life's circumstances can change, necessitating adjustments to one's spiritual routine. The goal should be to integrate meaningful and sustainable practices rather than overwhelming oneself with stringent requirements.

In conclusion, integrating spiritual practices into daily life can transform mundane routines into profound spiritual engagements, enriching one's life and fostering a deeper connection with the divine. By incorporating practices like meditation, prayer, engagement with spiritual texts, and community participation, individuals can find spiritual sustenance amid the chaos of everyday life. These practices offer a pathway to greater peace, understanding, and fulfillment, contributing to a balanced and meaningful life. As more individuals embrace these practices, the collective spiritual health of communities can also improve, creating a more compassionate and mindful society.

CHAPTER VI

Challenges and Pitfalls in Spiritual Intimacy

Addressing Common Misconceptions and Challenges

Spiritual intimacy is an essential aspect of holistic personal development and a deeply rooted component of many platonic and romantic relationships. Yet, despite its significance, it is often misunderstood and riddled with misconceptions that can hinder individuals from truly embracing its benefits. This section explores some of these common misunderstandings and the challenges associated with spiritual intimacy, offering insights into the way they can be effectively addressed.

One of the primary misconceptions about spiritual intimacy is that it solely pertains to religious activities or practices. Many people associate spirituality exclusively with organized religion, such as attending church or participating in religious rituals. However, spiritual intimacy extends beyond these boundaries to include any practices that inspire connection to something greater than oneself, which can be nature, art, meditation, or thoughtful conversation. This broader understanding allows individuals to explore spiritual intimacy regardless of their religious beliefs or lack thereof. To address this misconception, educators and communicators must redefine spirituality in inclusive terms, highlighting its universal, personal nature that transcends specific religious frameworks.

Another challenge is the belief that spiritual intimacy can only be achieved with a partner who has identical spiritual beliefs or practices. This notion can prevent meaningful connections and discourage the exploration of spiritual intimacy in diverse relationships. In truth, spiritual intimacy thrives on the principles of respect, openness, and genuine curiosity about others' beliefs and values. Couples or friends do not need to share the same spiritual paths to experience profound spiritual closeness; they need to share a mutual willingness to understand and support each other's spiritual journeys. Encouraging dialogues about spirituality that respect individual differences can enhance mutual understanding and intimacy in a relationship.

There is also a misconception that spiritual intimacy is inherently peaceful and harmonious. While it can be profoundly comforting and unifying, like any form of intimacy, it can also involve conflict and discomfort. When individuals open up spiritually, they reveal their most vulnerable beliefs about the meaning of life, the universe, and personal values, which can lead to disagreements or emotional clashes. However, these challenges should not be seen as deterrents but as opportunities for deeper understanding and growth. Couples and friends might need guidance to navigate these waters effectively. Through tools such as active listening, conflict resolution skills, and empathy, people can learn to use these experiences to strengthen their relationships rather than weaken them.

Additionally, the challenge of developing spiritual intimacy often lies in the modern lifestyle, which is predominantly fast-paced and centered around material achievements. Many individuals find it difficult to allocate time for spiritual growth and intimate conversations amid daily responsibilities. This issue can be addressed by consciously making time for spirituality in one's schedule, whether it is through meditation, reflective reading, nature walks, or shared experiences that foster deeper discussions about life's bigger questions. Prioritizing these practices can help individuals and couples integrate spiritual intimacy into their regular routine, making it a nourishing component of their relationships and personal well-being.

Moreover, there is a prevalent belief that spiritual intimacy requires a certain level of spiritual knowledge or expertise, which can intimidate those who feel they are not "spiritual enough" to engage in such interactions. This can establish a barrier to entry for many people who might otherwise benefit from exploring spiritual dimensions of intimacy. Demystifying spirituality and promoting an understanding that everyone is on a unique spiritual journey can help alleviate these fears. Resources such as workshops, books, and community groups can be significant in providing accessible opportunities for learning and exploration without the pressure of having to reach a certain spiritual threshold.

Finally, a significant challenge in nurturing spiritual intimacy is the discomfort with vulnerability that many people experience. Sharing one's spiritual beliefs involves a level of openness that can feel risky or uncomfortable in a world where such topics are often viewed as private or sensitive. To cultivate a safer environment for these exchanges, individuals must work towards building trust and demonstrating non-judgmental acceptance in their interactions. Establishing ground rules for discussions about spirituality that include confidentiality and a clear understanding that the goal is to listen and understand rather than to agree or convince can also help participants feel more secure.

In conclusion, spiritual intimacy is a complex and richly rewarding aspect of human relationships that is often fraught with misconceptions and challenges. By broadening the definition of spirituality to include various forms of connection, embracing differences in spiritual paths, understanding the role of conflict in growth, integrating spiritual practices into everyday life, reducing the barriers to spiritual engagement, and fostering a culture of trust and openness, individuals can overcome these hurdles. This approach enhances personal spiritual growth and strengthens the bonds between individuals, allowing them to share a deeply fulfilling and profoundly intimate aspect of their lives. Through education, dialogue, and practice, the misconceptions surrounding spiritual intimacy can be dismantled, paving the way for more inclusive and supportive spiritual communities.

Navigating Differences in Sexual Desire and Spiritual Beliefs

In the intricate dance of intimate relationships, couples often encounter the challenge of aligning their sexual desires with their spiritual beliefs. These differing aspects can significantly affect spiritual intimacy, which encompasses a deep, shared connection that transcends the physical to include emotional, mental, as well as spiritual unity. This section delves into how couples can navigate the complex interplay between sexual desire and spiritual beliefs to foster a more profound spiritual intimacy.

Sexual desire and spiritual beliefs are both fundamental aspects of human identity, but they follow different trajectories and principles that can sometimes conflict. For many, sexual desire is a natural and important expression of love and intimacy that strengthens the bond between partners. However, when partners have different levels of sexual desire or different understandings of the role sex should play in their relationship, it can lead to feelings of rejection, inadequacy, or guilt. This is especially true when these differences are intertwined with varying spiritual beliefs that may prescribe specific behaviors or boundaries around sexuality.

One common challenge is when one partner views their sexual desires as a significant part of their spiritual expression—seeing the physical union as a manifestation of their love and spiritual connection—while the other may hold a more restrained view perhaps influenced by religious teachings that might emphasize purity, modesty, or the sanctification of sexual relations within certain limits. These divergent views can create a tension that is not easily reconciled and can strain both the relationship and the individual's spiritual peace.

To navigate these differences effectively, it is crucial for couples to engage in open, honest, and empathetic communication. Each partner needs to feel safe enough to express their needs, desires, and beliefs without fear of judgment. This involves creating a dialogue that respects boundaries and seeks to understand rather than to persuade or convert. For instance, discussing how each partner's spiritual beliefs impact their view of sexual intimacy can help illuminate underlying values and forge a shared understanding or identify areas where compromise might be found.

In addition to communication, education plays a pivotal role in harmonizing differences in sexual desire and spiritual beliefs. Partners can benefit from educating themselves about each other's spiritual traditions and the teachings related to sexuality within those traditions. This knowledge can demystify misconceptions, reduce biases, and foster a greater appreciation for the partner's perspective. Couples might find it helpful to attend workshops or counseling sessions that focus on integrating spirituality and sexuality. These programs can offer practical tools and frameworks for aligning differing sexual desires with spiritual practices, thus enhancing intimacy.

Moreover, it is beneficial for partners to explore new spiritual practices that embrace both their needs. This might involve meditation, prayer, or rituals symbolically representing their union and shared spiritual path. Such practices can act as a bridge between differing levels of desire and disparate spiritual ideologies. They provide a shared space where both partners can connect spiritually and sexually, honoring their intimate bond while nurturing their individual spiritual growth.

Therapeutic intervention may also be necessary when differences are particularly entrenched or when they cause significant distress. Sex therapists or relationship counselors skilled in addressing both spiritual and sexual issues can offer guidance. These professionals can help couples explore their expectations and assumptions about sex and spirituality, and work through feelings of shame or guilt that may arise from conflicting desires and beliefs.

Another key technique is the practice of mindfulness, which involves present moment awareness without judgment. Mindfulness can enhance emotional connection and sexual intimacy by helping partners become more attuned to their own and each other's needs and emotions. Practicing mindfulness together can lead to deeper empathy, reduced stress, and a greater capacity for both partners to express their desires in ways that are respectful and affirming of each other's spiritual beliefs.

Patience and compromise are essential as partners navigate this journey. Differences in sexual desire and spiritual beliefs are unlikely to be resolved quickly. Instead, approaching these differences as a continual process of learning and adaptation can help maintain the relationship's health. Partners should be prepared to revisit discussions about their needs and boundaries as their relationship and individual spiritual journeys evolve.

In conclusion, navigating differences in sexual desire and spiritual beliefs within the context of spiritual intimacy requires a multifaceted approach that includes open communication, education, mutual exploration of new spiritual practices, professional guidance, mindfulness, and an ongoing commitment to compromise and understanding. By addressing these differences head-on and viewing them as opportunities for growth, couples can enhance their relationship both sexually and spiritually. This balanced integration of sexuality and spirituality not only deepens intimacy but also enriches the couple's connection to each other and the divine. Through patient and persistent efforts, partners can achieve a harmonious alignment that celebrates both their physical and spiritual unions.

Overcoming Cultural and Religious Barriers

In a world as diverse and interconnected as ours, intimate relationships often cross cultural and religious boundaries, presenting unique challenges that can impact the depth and quality of spiritual intimacy. Spiritual intimacy involves a shared sense of connection that transcends the physical, touching upon each individual's core beliefs and values. This section explores the complexities of overcoming cultural and religious barriers in spiritual intimacy, offering insights into how couples can bridge these divides to foster a deeper, more meaningful connection.

Cultural and religious differences can profoundly influence how individuals perceive and practice spirituality. These differences often encompass fundamental beliefs about the purpose of life, the nature of the divine, moral values, rituals, and practices. When partners hail from different spiritual or cultural backgrounds, these discrepancies can lead to misunderstandings and conflicts that strain the relationship. The challenge, therefore, is not only to bridge gaps in understanding but also to forge a path that respects and celebrates these differences.

The first step in overcoming these barriers is through open and honest communication. Partners need to express their beliefs, values, and practices without fear of judgment. This conversation should aim not to convert or persuade but to understand and appreciate the spiritual heritage of each other. By doing so, couples can identify common ground and areas of difference, which is crucial for navigating their spiritual journey together. Effective communication involves active listening, where each partner pays close attention to what the other is saying and reflects on it thoughtfully, demonstrating respect and empathy.

Education plays a crucial role in bridging cultural and religious divides. Understanding each partner's beliefs' historical, social, and theological contexts can demystify seemingly strange or unfamiliar practices and ideologies. This understanding can be fostered through reading, attending workshops, visiting religious services together, and engaging in discussions with knowledgeable individuals from both backgrounds. Through education, partners can advocate for each other's traditions, strengthening the bond and enhancing spiritual intimacy.

Creating new traditions can also help overcome cultural and religious barriers. While respecting and incorporating elements from each partner's background, couples can develop unique rituals reflecting a shared spiritual vision. These might include celebrating holidays from both traditions, creating a blended prayer or meditation routine, or even developing a new set of rituals that honor both cultures equally. These shared practices can act as a foundation for a jointly built spiritual life, reinforcing the couple's unity and commitment to each other's spiritual well-being.

Moreover, professional guidance from counselors who specialize in interfaith or intercultural relationships can be invaluable. These professionals can provide the tools and strategies to address sensitive issues related to doctrinal conflicts, family pressures, and societal expectations. Counseling can help partners navigate the complexities of integrating different spiritual landscapes, ensuring that each person's beliefs are treated with dignity and respect.

Flexibility and compromise are essential qualities that partners need to cultivate actively. No two individuals from the same culture or religion will have identical beliefs and practices. Recognizing that compromise does not mean abandonment of one's beliefs but rather a harmonious adjustment that enhances mutual spiritual growth is vital. This adjustment might involve alternating between different modes of spiritual expression or finding neutral spiritual activities that both can share enthusiastically.

Another significant challenge is dealing with external pressures from family and community, which can intensify cultural and religious differences. Couples may face resistance or outright opposition, which can strain their relationship and make spiritual intimacy difficult to achieve. Building a strong support network that includes open-minded and supportive friends, family members, or community groups is crucial to combat this. This network can provide encouragement, advice, and a safe space to nurture the couple's joint spiritual path.

In conclusion, overcoming cultural and religious barriers to achieve spiritual intimacy is not merely about resolving differences but about embracing them as opportunities for growth and deeper understanding. Through open communication, education, the creation of new traditions, professional guidance, flexibility, compromise, and the support of a like-minded community, couples can build a robust spiritual connection that transcends cultural and religious divides. This journey, while challenging, enriches the relationship and contributes to a more inclusive and empathetic world. Ultimately, the goal is to celebrate not just what is common but also what is unique in each partner's spiritual landscape, thereby fostering an intimacy that is both spiritually profound and culturally rich.

Maintaining Boundaries and Consent in Spiritual Relationships

In the context of spiritual relationships, maintaining boundaries and ensuring consent are paramount for fostering a healthy, respectful, and nurturing environment. Spiritual relationships, whether they involve a mentor and mentee, spiritual director and seeker, or members of a spiritual community, require profound trust and openness, which can only be achieved through clear boundaries and mutual consent. This section explores the importance of these elements, strategies for their implementation, and the benefits of their proper management in spiritual contexts.

Boundaries in spiritual relationships help define the limits and expectations of the interaction. Without clear boundaries, these relationships can become sources of confusion, misconduct, and emotional distress. This is particularly crucial in relationships involving a power differential, such as between a spiritual leader and a congregant, where the potential for abuse of power can be significant. Boundaries protect both parties by clarifying what is acceptable within the relationship, thereby preventing misunderstandings and maintaining the dignity as well as respect of all involved.

Consent in spiritual relationships, while often discussed in the context of physical or sexual interactions, is equally vital in non-physical interactions. Consent involves ongoing communication about each person's wishes and comfort levels with various aspects of the spiritual relationship. It is crucial that all parties feel they can freely express when they are uncomfortable or wish to change the nature of their engagement without fear of judgment or retaliation. This aspect of consent is foundational to creating a safe space for spiritual growth as well as exploration.

One effective way to maintain boundaries and consent is to establish a clear framework or agreement at the outset. This agreement should outline the objectives of the relationship, the roles and responsibilities of each party, and the ethical standards to which they will adhere. For example, a spiritual director might use a formal agreement that specifies the confidentiality of their discussions, the regularity and duration of meetings, and a code of conduct that explicitly forbids any form of harassment or discrimination.

Education about boundaries and consent should be an ongoing component of all spiritual communities and relationships. Regular training sessions, workshops, and discussions can reinforce the importance of these concepts and provide updated information and strategies for handling boundary-related issues. Education empowers individuals to recognize and advocate for their boundaries and teaches leaders how to acknowledge and navigate the boundaries of others respectfully.

Transparency is another key element in maintaining healthy boundaries and consent. This means being open about one's intentions, changes in the relationship dynamics, and the processes in place for reporting and addressing grievances. Transparency builds trust and facilitates open dialogue, where concerns about boundaries or consent can be addressed promptly and effectively.

Moreover, maintaining professional behavior in spiritual relationships is essential. This includes avoiding dual relationships where the roles are mixed (such as being both a spiritual mentor and a business partner), which can confuse boundaries and complicate consent. If dual relationships are unavoidable, it is vital to establish evident boundaries to separate and manage the different interactions appropriately.

It is also essential to have systems in place for accountability. Spiritual leaders and mentors should be accountable to higher authorities or governing bodies within their organizations. These bodies should provide oversight and a mechanism for handling accusations or breaches of boundaries impartially and sensitively. Such systems help to prevent abuses of power and ensure that grievances are appropriately addressed, restoring trust and rectifying situations that may have harmed members.

Practicing reflexivity, or the regular examination of one's actions and their impacts, is crucial for everyone involved in a spiritual relationship. Leaders, in particular, should continuously reflect on their interactions and adjust their behaviors to better respect and uphold the boundaries and consent of those they guide. This practice not only helps in maintaining ethical standards but also in personal growth and spiritual authenticity.

When boundaries and consent are not properly maintained, the consequences can be severe, including emotional trauma, loss of faith, and community disputes. These adverse outcomes highlight the need for vigilance and proactive management of these issues. Conversely, when boundaries and consent are respected, they promote a healthy environment where individuals feel valued, safe, and free to explore their spirituality without coercion or fear.

In conclusion, maintaining boundaries and consent in spiritual relationships is fundamental to the health and integrity of any spiritual practice or community. By establishing clear guidelines, regularly educating all members, ensuring transparency and accountability, avoiding dual relationships, and practicing reflexivity, spiritual relationships can thrive in an atmosphere of mutual respect and trust. These practices protect individuals and enhance the spiritual vitality and credibility of the community as a whole. Through diligent application of these principles, spiritual relationships can be powerful conduits for personal growth and profound connection.

CHAPTER VII

Embracing Love, Pleasure, and Spirituality

Cultivating Love and Compassion in Sexual Relationships

Cultivating love and compassion in sexual relationships is vital for deepening bonds and enhancing mutual satisfaction. While grounded in physical intimacy, these relationships flourish most profoundly when enriched with the emotional and spiritual dimensions of love and compassion. This section explores the significance of these qualities in sexual relationships, practical ways to cultivate them, and the transformative impact they can have on both partners.

Love and compassion are not mere sentiments but active practices that can fundamentally alter how individuals interact with each other in a sexual context. Love in this framework extends beyond romantic feelings to encompass a genuine concern for the other's well-being, happiness, and growth. Compassion involves a deep understanding of the other's feelings and experiences and a desire to alleviate their suffering and contribute to their happiness. These elements create a nurturing environment conducive to emotional and physical intimacy.

One of the primary ways to cultivate love and compassion in sexual relationships is through open and honest communication. Partners should feel free to express their desires, fears, and boundaries without judgement. This communication should be ongoing and evolve as the relationship grows. By engaging in heartfelt discussions about their sexual needs and emotional desires, partners can better understand each other and adjust their behaviors to foster a more loving and supportive relationship.

Empathy is critical in this process. It allows partners to see and feel from the other's perspective, which is essential for building compassion. Practicing empathy involves listening attentively, validating the other's feelings, and responding with kindness and understanding, rather than judgment or indifference. When empathy is present, sexual encounters transform into a deeper expression of love, enhancing the emotional connection and satisfaction derived from the relationship.

Mindfulness is another crucial practice for cultivating love and compassion. Being fully present during intimate moments allows partners to connect more deeply, appreciate each other's needs and responses, and create a shared experience that transcends physical satisfaction. Mindfulness helps in recognizing the transient nature of negative emotions and fosters a more stable, centered approach to handling conflicts and misunderstandings, which are inevitable in any relationship.

In addition to emotional practices, physical expressions of love and compassion are equally important. This can include more affectionate touch, attentive and responsive sexual engagement, and actions that physically demonstrate care and consideration. These gestures affirm the emotional bonds and signal a commitment to the partner's happiness, strengthening the relationship.

Educational endeavors can also enhance love and compassion. Learning about each other's bodies, sexual responses, and preferences through books, workshops, or counseling can open new pathways for intimacy. This knowledge empowers partners to engage more fully and respectfully with each other, fostering a deeper appreciation and connection that enhances both love and compassion.

Couples should also consider regular evaluations of their relationship's health. This could involve setting aside time to reflect on their intimacy, discuss any issues that might have arisen, and celebrate achievements. Such reviews encourage continuous growth and learning within the relationship, helping to maintain the vitality of their emotional and sexual connection.

However, cultivating love and compassion is not without challenges. It requires continuous effort, a willingness to be vulnerable, and an openness to change. Partners may encounter personal insecurities or cultural pressures that skew perceptions of sexuality and relationships. Overcoming these challenges often necessitates personal development work as well as mutual support within the relationship.

Fostering love and compassion in sexual relationships has profound benefits. Studies have shown that emotionally supportive and compassionate relationships lead to greater sexual satisfaction, improved mental and physical health, and a higher overall quality of life. These relationships tend to be more resilient to stress and conflict, providing a stable foundation for long-term happiness and well-being.

In conclusion, cultivating love and compassion in sexual relationships is a dynamic and rewarding endeavor. It involves open and honest communication, empathy, mindfulness, physical affection, education, and regular reflection. While challenges exist, the benefits of a compassionate and loving sexual relationship are immense, including deeper intimacy, greater satisfaction, and enhanced personal growth. By prioritizing these qualities, couples can create a fulfilling and enduring bond that survives and thrives through life's complexities.

Finding Pleasure and Joy in Spiritual Intimacy

Spiritual intimacy represents a profound level of connection that transcends the physical and emotional to encompass the spiritual. It is a bond that enriches the lives of those who experience it, bringing with it immense pleasure and joy. This section explores the nature of spiritual intimacy, its importance, and practical ways to cultivate such a connection in relationships, enhancing the spiritual well-being of all involved.

Spiritual intimacy involves a shared experience of the sacred and the transcendent, where individuals feel profoundly connected to each other and a larger reality. This connection can involve shared religious beliefs, mutual participation in spiritual practices, or simply a communal appreciation of the profound mysteries of existence. Whatever the form, spiritual intimacy deepens the relationship, providing a fulfilling sense of unity that augments the joys and pleasures found in other forms of intimacy.

The significance of spiritual intimacy lies in its capacity to enrich relationships by introducing a dimension of depth and meaning that other forms of intimacy might not reach. It encourages partners to open up about their deepest beliefs, fears, and hopes. This vulnerability can be tremendously rewarding, as it fosters an environment of mutual trust as well as respect, where individuals feel seen and understood on a fundamental level. Such an environment is ripe for experiencing joy and pleasure, not just from physical or emotional, but from a profound spiritual connection.

Cultivating spiritual intimacy requires intention and effort, particularly in a world that often prioritizes material and superficial over the spiritual and meaningful. One effective approach is engaging in shared spiritual practices. This might include meditation, prayer, rituals, or attending services together. These activities can help synchronize partners' spiritual rhythms and deepen their connection, making the spiritual aspect a regular part of their intimacy.

Communication is another vital tool in developing spiritual intimacy. Discussing one's spiritual experiences and beliefs can be incredibly intimate in itself. Such discussions should aim to explore and understand rather than convince or convert, allowing each partner to be truthful about their spiritual journeys. This open line of communication can lead to greater empathy, reduced conflicts, and a shared language of spirituality that enhances the joy and pleasure of the relationship.

In addition to shared practices and communication, creating a sacred space can also facilitate spiritual intimacy. This space can be physical—a particular room or corner of the home dedicated to spiritual practices—or temporal, such as specific times set aside for engaging in spiritual activities together. A sacred space provides a tangible reminder of the couple's commitment to their spiritual life together and can be a haven of tranquility and intimacy against the stress of everyday life. Moreover,

it is important to incorporate elements of joy and pleasure directly into these spiritual practices. This might involve integrating music, art, or nature—elements that bring joy into other aspects of life—into spiritual routines. For instance, couples might choose to meditate in a beautiful natural setting or create art together as a form of spiritual expression. These activities can make spiritual practices more enjoyable and deeply satisfying, enhancing both the individual and shared aspects of spiritual life.

Spiritual intimacy can also be fostered through acts of service. Engaging together in community service or other altruistic activities can create shared feelings of goodwill and fulfillment. These acts extend the couple's spiritual intimacy into a broader context, connecting them with others in meaningful ways and multiplying the joy they experience both individually and together.

It is crucial to approach differences in spirituality with openness and respect. Not all partners will share the same spiritual beliefs or practices, and these differences need not be an obstacle to spiritual intimacy. Instead, they can be viewed as opportunities to expand one's spiritual horizons and deepen the relationship by exploring new spiritual landscapes together. This respectful acknowledgment of differences can itself be a profound source of joy and pleasure, as it embodies the principles of love and acceptance.

The benefits of spiritual intimacy are manifold. It can provide a significant source of support during times of trouble, enhancing resilience against stress and adversity. It also enriches the relationship's emotional and physical intimacy, as the trust and connection built through spiritual closeness translate into greater openness and satisfaction in other areas of the relationship.

In conclusion, finding pleasure and joy in spiritual intimacy is a deeply enriching endeavor that transcends mere happiness to touch upon the sublime. It involves shared practices, open communication, the creation of a sacred space, integration of joyful elements, acts of service, and a respectful exploration of differences. Through these means, couples can enhance their relationship and connect to a greater spiritual reality, finding deep and lasting joy in the union of their spirits. Such intimacy fortifies them against the trials of life and enriches their daily existence with profound pleasure and fulfillment.

Balancing Physical and Spiritual Needs

Pursuing a balanced life that adequately addresses physical and spiritual needs is a significant endeavor that can enhance overall well-being and satisfaction. In a world that often emphasizes the material over the metaphysical, individuals can struggle to find a harmony that respects both aspects of existence. This section explores the importance of balancing physical and spiritual needs, the challenges inherent in this pursuit, and practical strategies for achieving a harmonious life.

Physical needs are those requirements necessary to maintain the health and functionality of the human body, including nutrition, exercise, rest, and medical care. Neglecting these basic needs can lead to many health problems that detract from one's quality of life and ability to pursue higher goals. Conversely, spiritual needs involve the quest for meaning, purpose, and connection that transcends the everyday physical aspects of life. This can include practices like meditation, prayer, religious worship, or simply contemplative reflection on one's place in the universe.

The importance of balancing these needs cannot be overstated. Excessive focus on physical needs without attending to spiritual development can lead to a life that feels empty and unfulfilled, regardless of physical health or wealth. On the other hand, overly prioritizing spiritual pursuits at the expense of physical health can undermine spiritual growth and lead to physical suffering, which can distract and detract from spiritual pursuits. A balanced approach that nurtures both body and soul is essential for holistic health and happiness.

Challenges to achieving this balance are manifold. Modern lifestyles, especially in industrialized nations, often stress productivity and physical acquisition, which can overshadow spiritual development. Many people find themselves trapped in routines that prioritize work and material accumulation, leaving little time or energy for spiritual pursuits. Additionally, consumer culture promotes a physicalist understanding of happiness that can obscure the importance of spiritual well-being.

To overcome these challenges, individuals must first recognize the value of both physical and spiritual well-being. This recognition involves understanding that true contentment and happiness derive from a harmony of body and spirit. Once this value is established, practical steps can be taken to balance these needs effectively.

One effective strategy is integrating spiritual practices into everyday life. For example, individuals can use daily activities such as eating or walking as opportunities for mindfulness practices. Mindful eating entails paying complete attention to the experience of eating and appreciating the flavors, textures, and origins of food, which enhances physical health while also cultivating spiritual awareness. Similarly, walking can be transformed into a meditative practice that provides physical exercise, calms the mind, and nurtures the spirit.

Setting aside specific times for spiritual activities is another crucial strategy. This could include regular meditation sessions, weekly worship services, or daily reading of spiritual texts. Scheduling these activities ensures that they are not neglected amidst the busyness of daily life. It is essential, however, that these practices not become just another task on a to-do list but a meaningful set of experiences that truly nurture the spirit.

Physical self-care is equally crucial in the pursuit of spiritual growth. This entails maintaining a healthy diet, regular physical activity, and adequate rest. These practices improve physical health and enhance mental clarity and emotional stability, providing a stronger foundation for spiritual development. For instance, yoga can be particularly effective as it offers physical exercise while also promoting relaxation and mindfulness.

In addition to personal practices, community involvement can help balance physical and spiritual needs. Engaging with a community that shares spiritual interests provides social support, vital for mental and physical health, and enhances spiritual growth through shared experiences and teachings. This can help individuals feel grounded and connected, further integrating their spiritual and physical lives.

Adapting to life's changing circumstances is also necessary for maintaining this balance. What works at one stage of life may not be appropriate in another, due to changes in health, responsibilities, or understanding. Flexibility and willingness to adjust one's approach to balancing physical and spiritual needs is key. This might mean altering one's physical activities as one ages or shifting one's spiritual practices in response to evolving beliefs or life situations.

In conclusion, balancing physical and spiritual needs is crucial for a holistic approach to health and well-being. This balance is not static but requires continual adjustment and integration based on personal growth and changing circumstances. Individuals are able to improve the quality of their life by employing practical strategies such as integrating spiritual practices into daily routines, prioritizing physical self-care, engaging with supportive communities, and remaining adaptable to life's changes. Successfully balancing these aspects allows for a fuller, more satisfying existence that honors both the body and the soul. Such a balanced approach fosters personal happiness and health and contributes to a more harmonious and mindful society.

Embracing Self-Love and Self-Care Practices

In the contemporary wellness landscape, the concepts of self-love and self-care have emerged as crucial elements for overall health and well-being. These practices are not merely indulgent; they are fundamental processes that enhance one's quality of life by fostering emotional, mental, and physical health. This section explores the importance of self-love and self-care, delineates various practical methods for implementing these practices, and discusses their transformative impact on personal growth and satisfaction.

Self-love is the foundation of self-care. It involves recognizing and respecting one's worth and well-being as paramount, manifesting in actions and thoughts that nurture one's health and happiness. Self-love motivates individuals to make beneficial choices in life, from the relationships they enter to how they manage stress and the priorities they set. It is known as a state of appreciation for oneself that rises from actions that support physical, psychological, as well as spiritual growth.

Self-care, conversely, is the mechanism by which self-love is practiced. It includes any intentional actions taken to care for physical, mental, and emotional health. Good self-care is key to enhanced mood as well as lessened anxiety. It's also key to a better relationship with oneself as well as others. Self-care means taking the time to do things that help you live well and improve both your physical and mental health. Whether it's through nourishing the body with healthy food, engaging in physical activities, getting enough rest, managing stress through mindfulness and meditation, or setting aside time for leisure and pleasure, self-care is vital for building resilience against stress and adversity.

The importance of these practices cannot be overstated. Incorporating self-love and self-care can be transformative in an era where burnout and stress are commonplace. These practices enhance one's ability to interact with the world more positively and productively. By ensuring that one's own needs are met, individuals are better equipped to meet the challenges of their daily lives with energy and enthusiasm. Moreover, self-love and self-care are acts of resistance against the often overwhelming demands of modern life, which frequently prioritizes productivity over well-being.

One effective self-care practice is the development of a balanced routine that includes adequate sleep, nutrition, exercise, and relaxation. Sleep is critical for mental clarity, emotional regulation, and physical health. Nutrition provides the necessary energy levels and biochemical inputs that are required for the body and brain to function at their best. Because exercise releases endorphins, which lessen pain and increase enjoyment, it is essential for both sustaining physical and mental health. Lastly, relaxation and leisure activities help to decrease stress and restore energy.

Meditation and mindfulness are also valuable self-care practices that improve mental health. They foster a heightened awareness of the present moment and help cultivate a state of mental clarity and calm. By practicing mindfulness, individuals can manage stress, enhance emotional reactivity, and improve concentration and cognitive function. Furthermore, meditation has been shown to decrease the density of brain tissue interconnected with anxiety and stress through neuroplasticity.

Another critical aspect of self-care is setting healthy boundaries. This means learning to say no when necessary, to avoid overcommitting, and to recognize when relationships are detrimental rather than supportive. Healthy boundaries help preserve emotional energy and promote emotional well-being by keeping stress levels in check and ensuring that one's own needs are prioritized.

Self-care also involves seeking professional help when necessary. Mental health is equally significant as physical health; sometimes professional intervention is needed to maintain or improve mental well-being. This might include therapy, counseling, or medical treatment, which should be viewed not as a failure to manage one's problems alone, but as a proactive step towards better health.

Journaling is another powerful self-care tool that can help individuals process emotions, reflect on their experiences, and gain clarity about their desires and needs. Writing can be therapeutic and is often used as a tool for emotional exploration as well as processing.

Furthermore, engaging with a community can significantly enhance the self-care process. Social support is vital for mental health, and engaging in group activities can provide a sense of belonging and connection. Whether it's through sports, clubs, or other social gatherings, being part of a community can mitigate feelings of loneliness and boost one's mood.

In conclusion, embracing self-love and self-care is essential for fostering well-being and enhancing one's quality of life. By understanding the intrinsic value of self-love and implementing practical self-care practices such as maintaining a balanced routine, practicing mindfulness, setting healthy boundaries, seeking professional help, journaling, and engaging with community activities, individuals can significantly improve their emotional, physical, and mental health. These practices enrich individual lives and contribute positively to the broader social environment, promoting a culture of health and well-being that benefits all.

CHAPTER VIII

The Future of Sexual Magic and Spiritual Intimacy

Trends and Innovations in Sacred Sexuality Practices

In recent years, there has been a noticeable shift in the cultural understanding and practice of sexuality, moving from a purely physical or recreational view to one that encompasses spiritual and holistic dimensions. Sacred sexuality—a term that refers to the integration of spirituality with sexual experience—aims to elevate sexuality from mere physical interactions to profound, meaningful exchanges that enrich both the body and soul. This section explores the latest trends as well as innovations in sacred sexuality practices, examining how they are reshaping intimate relationships and spiritual growth today.

Sacred sexuality is rooted in ancient practices found in various traditions, such as Tantra, Taoism, and the Kama Sutra. These traditions view sexual energy as a powerful force that can enhance spiritual enlightenment when harnessed correctly. These traditions teach that sexuality can transcend its physical dimensions to become a path to spiritual unity and personal transformation. The modern resurgence and innovation in these practices reflect a growing societal recognition of their potential for fostering deeper personal connections and achieving higher states of consciousness.

One significant trend in sacred sexuality is the increasing incorporation of mindfulness and meditation into sexual practices. Mindfulness involves a focused awareness on the present moment, and when applied to sexuality, it encourages individuals to engage deeply and wholly with their physical sensations and emotional responses. This practice enhances pleasure by increasing the intensity and awareness of physical sensations and promotes a deeper emotional connection between partners. Meditation can similarly transform sexual experiences by creating a calm, focused, and open environment where partners can connect without the distractions of everyday life.

Another innovation in this field is the use of technology to disseminate ancient knowledge and practices. With the rise of the internet as well as digital communication, teachings that were once accessible only to select groups or individuals in specific geographical regions are now available worldwide. Online workshops, virtual retreats, and digital courses on Tantra and other practices make it easier for individuals to explore sacred sexuality irrespective of their location. These resources often blend traditional teachings with contemporary approaches, making them relevant to modern audiences and addressing contemporary issues such as consent, gender identity, and sexual health.

Tantric yoga and energy work represent further areas where significant innovations are occurring. Tantric yoga, an ancient practice, uses specific asanas, breathwork, and meditation techniques to build and channel sexual energy through the body's chakras or energy centres. This practice is believed to improve physical and spiritual health by enhancing energetic flow and balance. Modern practitioners are adapting these techniques to suit individual needs and contemporary lifestyles, making them more accessible and applicable to everyday life.

Moreover, there is a growing trend toward the integration of Western therapeutic practices with sacred sexuality.

Psychotherapists and counselors are increasingly acknowledging the role of sexual health in overall mental health and are integrating techniques from sacred sexuality to help clients deal with issues such as sexual dysfunction, relationship problems, and past trauma. This holistic approach not only helps individuals and couples find healing but also enriches their understanding and experience of sexuality as a vital component of their well-being.

The practice of sacred sexuality is also expanding its reach through diverse community-based initiatives. Workshops, retreats, and seminars are increasingly common and are designed to cater to an array of demographics, including LGBTQ+ communities, people with disabilities, and those from various religious and cultural backgrounds. These initiatives aim to create inclusive, safe spaces where all individuals can explore their sexuality in a spiritually supportive environment.

Cultural integration is another innovative aspect of the modern sacred sexuality movement. Practitioners are blending elements from different traditions to create new, hybrid forms of sacred sexual practice that respect cultural differences while promoting universal values such as love, respect, and spiritual growth. These practices often emphasize the unifying power of sexuality to bridge cultural divides and promote peace and understanding among diverse populations.

In conclusion, the trends and innovations in sacred sexuality practices are diverse and widespread, reflecting a growing recognition of the spiritual dimensions of sexuality. By integrating ancient wisdom with modern techniques and technologies, these practices are becoming more accessible and applicable to a wider audience, fostering greater intimacy, healing, and spiritual growth. As society continues to evolve, sacred sexuality will likely play an increasingly significant part in shaping how individuals and communities understand and experience the profound connection between the spiritual as well as the physical. Through ongoing innovation and cultural integration, sacred sexuality promises to continue its evolution as a powerful tool for personal and societal transformation.

Integrating Technology and Tradition in Spiritual Connection

In the contemporary world, where the realms of technology and tradition often seem at odds, the integration of these domains within the context of spiritual practices presents both unique challenges and unprecedented opportunities. This fusion aims to enhance spiritual connection and understanding by leveraging modern technological advances alongside ancient spiritual traditions. This section explores the nuances of integrating technology with tradition in spirituality, examining the potential benefits, methods employed, and considerations that must be addressed to maintain the essence of spiritual practice.

The advancement of technology has dramatically transformed all aspects of human life, including how we explore and express our spirituality. Traditionally, spiritual practices have been transmitted orally or through written texts, and personal spiritual experiences have largely been facilitated through direct interaction with nature or within sacred spaces. However, with the rise of the internet and digital media, there is an increasing move towards digital spiritual experiences, which has both democratized and complicated the landscape of spiritual practice.

One significant benefit of integrating technology into spiritual practices is the increased accessibility it offers. People who cannot physically attend traditional places of worship or spiritual retreats can now participate in virtual sessions, which can be streamed live or recorded. This is particularly impactful for individuals with disabilities, those living in remote areas, or those in restrictive environments where certain practices may be frowned upon or outlawed. Technology thus serves as a bridge, providing widespread access to spiritual teachings and communities that were previously out of reach for many.

Moreover, technology facilitates a new form of the communal spiritual experience through online platforms. Social media groups, discussion forums, and virtual reality experiences offer new communal prayer, meditation, and discussion spaces, transcending geographical limitations. These virtual communities can promote a sense of belonging and support, mirroring traditional physical communities, but with the added advantage of connecting like-minded individuals from across the globe.

However, integrating technology into spiritual practices is not without its challenges. One of the major concerns is the potential dilution of the authenticity and sacredness of traditional practices. For instance, digital meditation apps might offer guided sessions that are accessible and user-friendly but can lack the personalized guidance and communal energy of meditating in a group within a sacred space. Therefore, it is crucial to approach technology integration with sensitivity and respect for the traditions being adapted. This includes ensuring that technological adaptations are developed in consultation with knowledgeable practitioners of the tradition.

Further, there is the challenge of commercialization. As spiritual practices become integrated with technology, there is a risk that these sacred traditions could be commodified. This commodification risks stripping practices of their spiritual depth and makes them subject to the whims of market dynamics, potentially prioritizing profitability over spiritual efficacy. To counteract this, developers and spiritual leaders must work together to preserve the core values and integrity of the spiritual practices.

To effectively integrate technology with tradition, innovative approaches are being employed. Augmented and virtual reality technologies are being explored for their potential to create immersive spiritual experiences. For example, virtual reality can simulate walking the Camino de Santiago, allowing users to experience this pilgrimage from their homes while accessing historical and spiritual insights along the way. Similarly, augmented reality apps can overlay traditional spiritual texts with interpretations and teachings, enhancing the user's understanding and engagement.

Another innovative integration is using data analytics and artificial intelligence to understand spiritual texts and practices. AI can examine vast amounts of data to uncover patterns, interpretations, and connections that might take scholars years to identify. These insights can then be used to develop more tailored and effective spiritual guidance, which can be disseminated through apps and websites.

Despite these innovations, maintaining a balance between technology and tradition involves ensuring that the use of technology enhances rather than replaces the personal, communal, and transcendent aspects of spirituality. This balance can be achieved by adopting a complementary approach where technology serves as a tool to facilitate traditional practices, not as an end in itself. For instance, while an app might guide an individual through a meditation practice, it should also encourage visits to a local meditation center or community group, thereby fostering a real-world spiritual community.

In conclusion, integrating technology and tradition in spiritual practices offers a promising avenue for enhancing spiritual connections in an increasingly digital world. By making spiritual practices more accessible, creating new forms of community, and offering innovative ways to engage with traditional teachings, technology has the potential to profoundly influence the spiritual landscape. However, this integration must be approached thoughtfully, with a steadfast commitment to preserving the authenticity and sacredness of traditional practices. Careful consideration and collaborative efforts between technologists and spiritual leaders can ensure that technology is a valuable ally in the quest for spiritual growth and understanding rather than a disruptive force. This balanced approach promises not only to maintain but to enrich the spiritual connections that are so vital to human life.

Building Communities and Support Networks for Spiritual Intimacy

In the journey of spiritual growth, the role of communities and support networks is indispensable. Spiritual intimacy, which refers to a deep, meaningful connection that transcends physical and emotional levels to touch the spiritual aspects of being, flourishes significantly within a supportive community context. This section explores the importance of building communities and support networks for enhancing spiritual intimacy, the strategies for fostering such environments, and their impact on individual and collective spiritual journeys.

The concept of spiritual intimacy involves more than personal spiritual practices; it extends to shared experiences and connections that reinforce individual and collective beliefs. These connections are often cultivated within communities and networks that provide a sense of belonging, understanding, and mutual support. In these spaces, individuals find emotional and social support and a platform for profound spiritual interaction and growth.

Communities play a critical role in spiritual development. They serve as a nurturing ground for spiritual intimacy by providing a structured space where individuals can explore spiritual concepts and practices together. This communal interaction enhances the participants' spiritual experiences through collective worship, study, and reflection, which are difficult to achieve in isolation. Moreover, spiritual communities often provide a sense of continuity and tradition, linking individuals to a broader historical context that enriches their personal spiritual practices.

These communities' support is not merely logistical but deeply emotional and spiritual. Members can share their spiritual struggles and insights, thereby gaining new perspectives and deepening their understanding. This collective wisdom is a powerful tool for overcoming personal challenges and enhancing one's spiritual journey. Furthermore, the accountability to a community or network motivates individuals to persist in their spiritual practices, contributing to spiritual discipline and growth.

Building an effective community or network for spiritual intimacy involves several strategic steps. The first is defining the shared values and beliefs that will form the community's foundation. This clarity helps attract individuals who are aligned with the community's objectives and facilitates a unified approach to spiritual exploration.

Another crucial strategy is inclusivity. Spiritual communities should strive to be welcoming spaces for individuals from diverse backgrounds. This diversity enriches the community by introducing a variety of spiritual perspectives and practices, thus broadening the communal experience of spirituality. Achieving this requires active efforts to eliminate barriers to participation, such as economic hurdles, language differences, and cultural biases.

Communication is also vital in building and maintaining healthy spiritual communities. Regular, open dialogue within the community helps prevent misunderstandings and conflicts and fosters a supportive atmosphere. This can be facilitated through regular meetings, social gatherings, and the use of digital platforms where community members can connect and share experiences.

Additionally, leadership in spiritual communities must be approached with care and integrity. Leaders should be spiritually knowledgeable and embody the principles of empathy, transparency, and inclusivity. Effective leadership inspires trust and respect, which are essential for deep spiritual intimacy within the community.

Digital platforms have become increasingly crucial in building and maintaining spiritual communities in the modern age. These platforms break geographical barriers, allowing people from different parts of the world to participate in shared spiritual practices and discussions. Websites, social media, and apps can provide resources for spiritual learning and spaces for virtual fellowship, which are particularly valuable for those who may not have access to physical spiritual communities. For

instance, many spiritual communities use webinars and live streams for teachings and meditations, and forums or social media groups for discussion and support. These tools facilitate ongoing engagement and provide a repository of spiritual knowledge that can be accessed at any time, enhancing the scope and depth of spiritual practice among community members.

The impact of well-structured communities and support networks on spiritual intimacy is profound. For many individuals, these communities become a spiritual family that provides support and understanding through life's challenges. The shared experiences within the community —be it through ritual, service, study, or fellowship—deepen the members' spiritual lives and provide a practical framework within which they can grow and flourish.

Moreover, the support network within these communities often plays a crucial role in individual healing processes. The spiritual intimacy developed through these relationships can help individuals overcome personal traumas and find deeper meaning and purpose in life. This healing is facilitated not only through direct support but also by the inclusive and accepting environment that these communities foster.

In conclusion, building communities and support networks is essential for cultivating spiritual intimacy. These communities provide crucial support, facilitate deeper understanding, and offer a shared space for spiritual practices that enrich the individual's spiritual journey. By strategically building inclusive, communicative, and well-led communities and leveraging modern digital tools, spiritual intimacy can be significantly enhanced. The profound impact of these communities on individual and collective spiritual growth underscores the importance of communal support in the spiritual landscape of the modern world. Through these networks, individuals can explore spiritual depths and connect with others on similar paths, creating rich, supportive environments that nurture the soul.

Personal Reflections and Looking Forward

Sexual magic and spiritual intimacy represent profound and often misunderstood facets of human connection that intertwine the physical with the spiritual, creating experiences that transcend ordinary perceptions of intimacy. This section delves into personal reflections on the nature of sexual magic, explores the complexities of cultivating spiritual intimacy, and contemplates the future of these practices in a rapidly evolving world.

Sexual magic, a term that resonates with mystique and depth, refers to the use of sexual energies to enhance spiritual growth and personal transformation. It is rooted in the notion that sexual energy is one of the most potent forces in the universe, capable of unlocking profound spiritual insights and manifesting significant life changes. The practice involves more than just physical interaction; it requires an intentional focus on merging the spiritual with the physical, where each act of intimacy is infused with specific intentions for spiritual growth or healing.

Reflecting on the journey of exploring sexual magic reveals a tapestry of growth, challenges, and profound revelations. Initially, the concept might come across as esoteric or shrouded in secrecy, often relegated to the fringes of spiritual practices. However, when approached with an open mind and a respectful heart, sexual magic can open pathways to deeper emotional connections and a more nuanced understanding of spiritual energies.

One of the primary insights from exploring sexual magic is the recognition of sexual energy as a dynamic and transformative force. When harnessed consciously, this energy can elevate experiences of intimacy to acts of spiritual communion and creation. The practice encourages participants to engage with each other and the universe in a deeply reverent and purposefully transcendent manner, moving beyond the limitations of traditional romantic or sexual relationships.

Cultivating spiritual intimacy is an intricate process that necessitates vulnerability, honesty, and a profound commitment to personal and mutual growth. Spiritual intimacy extends beyond physical or even emotional connection; it encompasses a shared journey towards understanding and embodying spiritual truths, which can significantly enhance the relationship dynamics.

Developing this form of intimacy often involves regular spiritual practices that both partners engage in, such as meditation, ritualistic sexual practices, or shared prayer. These practices help in aligning spiritual intentions and deepen the relational connection, making every interaction an opportunity for spiritual enrichment. Moreover, the journey of cultivating spiritual intimacy is marked by continuous learning and adaptation, as each partner navigates their own spiritual paths while synchronizing their growth with each other.

Engaging in sexual magic and developing spiritual intimacy are not without challenges. One of the most significant hurdles is the societal misunderstanding and stigma associated with integrating sexuality and spirituality. These practices are often viewed through a lens of skepticism or moral judgment, which can create external pressures and personal doubts. Furthermore, finding a compatible partner who shares a similar spiritual outlook and openness to exploring sexual magic can be difficult, potentially leading to feelings of isolation or frustration.

Additionally, the deep level of vulnerability required in these practices can be daunting. Opening up spiritual and emotional spaces to another individual involves significant trust and the risk of emotional exposure, which can be intimidating and requires a strong foundation of communication and respect.

Looking forward, the landscape of sexual magic and spiritual intimacy appears poised for broader exploration and acceptance as societal attitudes continue to evolve. Increasing awareness and understanding of alternative spiritual practices, fueled by digital media and greater cultural exchanges, suggest that more individuals are beginning to recognize the value and legitimacy of integrating sexual and spiritual energies.

The future of these practices may involve a more structured approach to education and dissemination of knowledge, with potential for workshops, retreats, and online platforms dedicated to teaching interested individuals about the safe and respectful practice of sexual magic. This educational approach could help demystify the practices and make them accessible to a wider audience, promoting a more inclusive and holistic understanding of sexuality and spirituality.

Moreover, as research into the psychological and physiological impacts of spiritual practices expands, there could be a greater scientific understanding that supports the benefits of sexual magic and spiritual intimacy. This research has the potential to further validate these practices and encourage their integration into mainstream approaches to relationship counseling and personal development.

In conclusion, the journey of exploring sexual magic and cultivating spiritual intimacy is deeply personal and richly rewarding. It offers a unique blend of physical pleasure and spiritual growth, providing a fuller, more integrated approach to understanding human experiences and connections. While challenges and misunderstandings persist, the forward path promises greater exploration and acceptance as cultural perceptions continue to evolve.

As we look to the future, embracing these practices requires an open heart and mind, willingness to engage deeply with oneself and one's partner, and a commitment to navigating the complexities of integrating the physical with the spiritual. With continued education, respectful practice, and an open dialogue about the benefits and challenges, sexual magic and spiritual intimacy can provide profound insights and experiences that enrich our lives in unimaginable ways. This journey enhances personal and relational growth and contributes to a broader cultural shift towards a more inclusive and spiritually aware society.

CHAPTER IX

Reflection

Recapitulation of Key Concepts and Insights

Mystic love represents a profound, often transcendental expression of love that seeks to connect the deepest aspects of the human experience with the divine or the universal. It transcends traditional understandings of romantic or platonic love, aiming to reach an understanding of love as a powerful, spiritual force that moves beyond the personal to the cosmic. This section recaps the key concepts and insights related to exploring mystic love, drawing on spiritual traditions, philosophical reflections, and contemporary interpretations to illuminate this complex phenomenon.

Mystic love is an ancient yet perpetually fresh idea, found in the mystic traditions of numerous cultures and religions, from the Sufis of Islam, who speak of divine love as the ultimate connection between the soul and God, to the Christian mystics such as St. John of the Cross and his dark night of the soul, which articulates a journey towards divine union through love's purifying trials. In Hinduism, the concept of Bhakti (devotional love) carries similar mystical connotations, proposing a form of love that completely absorbs the devotee into the divine essence. Despite the diversity in these traditions, common to all is the belief that mystic love is a transformative, elevating force that not only intensifies one's relationship with the divine but also deepens one's understanding and connection with the universe and with other beings.

Philosophically, mystic love challenges the conventional frameworks of understanding love by proposing that true love is not merely an emotional state but a state of being that transcends the ego and individual self. It is seen as a pathway to enlightenment, where the lover and the beloved merge in a union that dissolves the illusions of separateness. This perspective is mirrored in the works of mystics such as Rumi, whose poems articulate the dissolution of personal identity in the fire of divine love.

Spiritually, mystic love is explored through practices that aim to dissolve the boundaries between the self and the other, between humanity and divinity. These practices might include meditation, prayer, contemplative reflection, and acts of extreme devotion and service. These practices aim to achieve an experiential understanding of love as a radical form of communion and communication with all that exists.

In contemporary times, mystic love has been subject to both revival and reinterpretation. Modern spiritual seekers and thinkers have been attracted to mystic love for its promise of deeper authenticity and connection in an often superficial world. Contemporary mystics and spiritual teachers have adapted ancient practices to modern contexts, emphasizing personal transformation through love and the breaking down of internal barriers to loving fully and profoundly.

However, exploring mystic love in the modern world presents specific challenges. Contemporary society's materialistic focus often relegates love to the realms of the sentimental or romantic, obscuring its deeper, transformative potentials. Moreover, the individualistic ethos prevalent today can make the dissolution of ego, which mystic love requires, particularly challenging. Mystic love demands a counter-cultural embrace of self-transcendence and a radical openness to the other that goes against the grain of much modern thinking and living.

Exploring mystic love offers several key insights into the nature of love and existence. Firstly, it reveals love as a force of unity and connectivity. In the mystic view, to love is to recognize and experience the inherent unity of all life, which directly challenges the modern perception of the world as fragmented and divided. This has profound implications for how individuals relate to each other and to the world at large, suggesting new paths for overcoming division and conflict through a love-based approach to living.

Secondly, mystic love highlights the journey of love as one of ongoing transformation and growth. Unlike conventional views of love as a state to be maintained, mystic love is dynamic, constantly evolving and deepening. This perspective encourages a view of personal and relational development that is always in process, always moving toward greater depths and higher states of understanding.

Thirdly, the pursuit of mystic love can lead to greater personal and spiritual resilience. By connecting individuals to a larger purpose and embedding them in a supportive context of meaning, mystic love can help people navigate the difficulties of life with greater composure and purpose. It offers a wellspring of strength and renewal that can be particularly valuable in times of personal or collective crisis.

As we move forward, the exploration of mystic love likely will continue to evolve and respond to the needs and conditions of the contemporary world. This might involve greater technology integration with mystic practices, making the insights of mystic love more accessible to a broader audience. It could also see a deeper dialogue between different religious and spiritual traditions on the nature of love, promoting a more inclusive and holistic view of mystic love that can bridge cultural and spiritual divides.

Furthermore, in an era marked by division and uncertainty, the principles of mystic love could offer valuable social and personal healing strategies. By promoting a view of love as inclusive, transformative, and enlightening, the teachings of mystic love provide pathways for individual fulfilment and collective peace and well-being.

In conclusion, mystic love remains a powerful and relevant concept for understanding and experiencing love in a profound, spiritually enriched way. As we recapitulate its key concepts and insights, we find a vision of love that transcends traditional boundaries and offers deep, substantive engagements with the divine and the cosmos. Moving forward, the difficulty will be to continue adapting this vision to the evolving needs of humanity, finding in mystic love not only personal solace and transformation but also insights that can address the broader ailments of our world. Through this, mystic love promises a deeper connection for individuals and a renewed basis for universal harmony and peace.

Final Thoughts on the Journey of Exploring Mystic Love

As we conclude our exploration of mystic love, we reflect on a journey that delves deep into the confluence of spirituality and profound affection, where love transcends the personal and touches the universal. This journey, rich in its complexity and sublime aspirations, offers transformative insights into the nature of love and the essence of human spiritual experience. This section provides final thoughts on the nuances, challenges, and profound truths encountered in pursuing mystic love, and contemplates the broader implications for individual and collective well-being.

At its core, mystic love is about connection — a deep, pervasive union that blurs the boundaries between the self and the other, the human and the divine. It embodies a love that is not confined by conventional romantic or filial bonds but is expansive, encompassing all of creation. This love suggests a pathway to understanding the universe not through intellect alone but through the heart, which recognizes other souls and the divine as part of a singular, interconnected whole.

The essence of mystic love is captured in the profound experiences of mystics across various religious traditions, from the ecstatic poems of Rumi and the passionate songs of Mirabai to the mystical writings of St. Teresa of Avila as well as the contemplative prayers of St. Francis of Assisi. These mystics did not merely write about love; they lived it as a radical form of spiritual practice that challenged and transcended the societal norms of their times. Their lives and works illuminate the journey of mystic love as one of intense personal transformation that demands courage, total surrender, and a willingness to embrace the unknown.

The path of mystic love is not without its challenges. One of the primary difficulties faced by those who walk this path is the profound sense of alienation that can arise when traditional societal and religious structures no longer suffice to contain their expanding spiritual experiences. The mystic's journey can be solitary, as the depth of their love and the radical nature of their spiritual insights often set them apart from mainstream society and sometimes even from their religious communities.

Additionally, the journey involves navigating the dark night of the soul, a term coined by St. John of the Cross to describe a period of spiritual desolation in which one feels utterly abandoned by the divine. This dark night is a crucial phase of the mystical journey, where the soul is purified, and the ego is dismantled, but it is a time fraught with doubt, fear, and profound suffering.

Despite these challenges, the journey of mystic love is ultimately about integration and acceptance. It calls for integrating the spiritual and the mundane, the divine and the earthly. This integration is not a rejection of the physical world but a full embrace of it, with a recognition that the divine permeates all things. Mystic love teaches that spiritual enlightenment does not necessitate renunciation of the world, but a deeper engagement with it, motivated by profound love and compassion.

Acceptance is also a key theme — acceptance of oneself, of others, and of the world in all its imperfection. Mystic love fosters a non-judgmental, embracing view of life that transcends personal prejudices and biases. This all-encompassing acceptance is crucial for promoting peace, both within one's own heart and in the world at large.

Exploring mystic love has significant implications for personal and collective well-being. On a personal level, this journey offers a path to deep inner peace and fulfillment that does not depend on external circumstances. It promotes emotional resilience and a profound sense of purpose, anchoring individuals in a love that is steadfast and transformative.

On a collective level, the principles of mystic love can revolutionize societal structures by promoting a worldview that emphasizes interconnectedness and compassion over competition and division. In a world rife with conflict and misunderstanding, mystic love offers a blueprint for building more harmonious communities grounded in mutual respect and caring.

As we look forward, the journey of exploring mystic love remains as relevant today as it has ever been. In an era characterized by materialism and disconnection, the call to explore a love that transcends the ego and seeks union with the divine is both radical and necessary. It challenges us to rethink our relationships, communities, and purposes.

Educational systems, spiritual organizations, and even political structures stand to benefit immensely from incorporating the insights of mystic love. By fostering an ethos that prioritizes deep, authentic connections over superficial interactions, we can cultivate a society that values spiritual wisdom and is more equitable and just.

The journey of mystic love is not an easy one, nor is it quick. It demands dedication, perseverance, as well as a willingness to be transformed from the inside out. However, the rewards it offers are profound and essential for the healing and elevation of the human spirit. As we continue to explore this mystical path, we do so with the hope that each step taken in love brings us closer to a more compassionate and spiritually fulfilled world.

In conclusion, exploring mystic love is a transformative journey that challenges individuals to seek a deeper, more inclusive understanding of love. It offers significant rewards for personal growth and collective well-being, promising a pathway to a more compassionate and spiritually attuned society. Through the continual pursuit of this profound love, we can hope to achieve not only personal enlightenment but also a universal harmony that resonates with the deepest truths of our existence. As we reflect on these final thoughts, let us move forward with the courage to embrace the mysteries of love in all its forms, fostering a world rich in spiritual intimacy and mystic beauty.

Encouragement for Further Exploration and Growth

The journey into the realms of mystic love is marked by profound transformation, deepening understanding, and expanding one's own spiritual horizons. It is a path that invites the seeker to transcend ordinary experiences of love, to delve into the depths of what it means to connect with the divine through the most powerful human emotion. This exploration is not just a passage through ancient texts or mystical traditions but a vibrant, living journey that continues to evolve with each individual's experience. This section aims to encourage further exploration and growth in the pursuit of mystic love, highlighting the transformative potential it holds for personal development and the enrichment of the human spirit.

At the heart of mystic love lies the potential for profound personal transformation. This form of love challenges individuals to look beyond the ego and the confines of self-centered desires, inviting them into a broader understanding of love as an expansive, universal force. By engaging with mystic love, seekers are prompted to question their preconceptions and to open their hearts to the possibility of a love that transcends physical and emotional boundaries, reaching into the spiritual essence of existence.

The exploration of mystic love is not a destination but a journey of continual growth and discovery. It requires an openness to new ideas, practices, and perspectives. This journey can be enriched by studying mystical texts from various spiritual traditions, engaging in practices that foster spiritual intimacy, and participating in communities that support these explorations. Through these avenues, seekers can gain insights into the diverse expressions of mystic love across cultures and epochs, expanding their understanding and deepening their connection to the divine.

Personal practice plays a crucial role in the exploration of mystic love. Meditation, prayer, contemplation, and acts of unconditional kindness are just a few examples of practices that can cultivate a direct experience of mystic love. These practices help to quiet the mind, open the heart, and foster a sense of connectedness with something greater than oneself. They also serve as a foundation for personal resilience, equipping individuals with the inner strength to navigate the challenges as well as uncertainties of life with grace and compassion.

Spiritual communities offer valuable support and guidance on the journey of exploring mystic love. These communities can provide a sense of belonging, opportunities for shared learning, and a collective energy that amplifies individual efforts. Engaging with such communities, whether in person or online, allows seekers to share their experiences, challenges, and insights, fostering a collective growth that benefits the individual and the wider community.

It is essential to acknowledge that the journey into mystic love may encounter obstacles and challenges. Doubts, misunderstandings, and periods of spiritual dryness are not uncommon. However, these challenges are integral to the process, offering opportunities for deeper reflection, learning, and growth. Perseverance and a compassionate and patient approach to oneself are essential. It is through facing and overcoming these challenges that the seeker's commitment is tested and their understanding deepened.

Compassion and self-love are foundational to the exploration of mystic love. By cultivating compassion for oneself and others, individuals can overcome barriers of judgment and separation, opening the way to a more inclusive and unconditional form of love. Self-love is equally essential, as it establishes a foundation of self-respect and worthiness that supports the opening of the heart to the divine love that mystic traditions speak of.

To those embarking on or continuing the journey of exploring mystic love, let this be an encouragement to delve deeper into the mysteries of love and spirit. Remember that each step taken in love, no matter how small, contributes to unfolding a larger journey towards understanding and unity. Be open to the lessons that love offers, willing to transform and be transformed by its power.

Let the exploration of mystic love be a source of inspiration, a path to healing, and a beacon of hope. It invites us to envision a world where love transcends all boundaries, fostering a more profound connection among all beings. The journey of mystic love is a call to awaken to the potential within each person to love profoundly and unconditionally, illuminating the way toward a more compassionate and spiritually enriched life.

In conclusion, exploring mystic love is a dynamic and evolving journey that offers rich personal and spiritual growth opportunities. It challenges seekers to expand their understanding of love, engage in practices that cultivate spiritual intimacy, and contribute to creating a world grounded in compassion and unity. As we encourage further exploration and growth in this realm, let us do so with open hearts, eager minds, and the courage to embrace the transformative power of mystic love.

CONCLUSION

As we reach the culmination of our exploration into the realms of sexual magic and spiritual intimacy, it is fitting to pause and reflect on the journey we have undertaken together. In "Mystic Love," we have traversed ancient wisdom traditions, delved into modern practices, and embarked on a quest to uncover the transformative potential inherent in the union of sexuality and spirituality. Now, as we bid farewell to this book, we find ourselves standing at the threshold of a new beginning — a beginning marked by integration, expansion, and a deepening sense of connection to ourselves, to others, and to the world around us.

Throughout our journey, we have encountered a wealth of insights, practices, and teachings that have challenged our preconceptions, expanded our awareness, and invited us to embrace new ways of being in the world. From the profound wisdom of tantra to the transformative power of ritual and symbolism, we have discovered a myriad of tools and techniques for cultivating spiritual intimacy and harnessing the energy of sexual magic for personal growth and healing.

Yet, perhaps the most profound revelation of our journey is the recognition that mystic love is not merely a destination to be reached, but a journey to be lived—a journey that unfolds in each moment, in each breath, and in each intimate encounter with ourselves and with others. It is a journey of integration, as we learn to embrace the full spectrum of our human experience—the light and the shadow, the pleasure and the pain, the ecstasy and the heartbreak. It is a journey of expansion, as we open ourselves to the infinite possibilities that arise when we surrender to the wisdom of the heart and the guidance of the soul.

As we take our leave from these pages, we carry with us a deeper understanding of the profound connection between sexuality and spirituality, and a renewed sense of reverence for the mysteries of love and intimacy. We also carry with us a profound sense of gratitude—for the teachers who have illuminated our path, for the companions who have walked beside us, and for the wisdom that has guided us on our journey.

But our journey does not end here. It is merely a beginning marked by the realization that mystic love is not confined to the pages of a book or the walls of a temple, but is woven into the fabric of our everyday lives, waiting to be discovered in the most ordinary of moments. It is a journey that calls us to embody the principles of love, compassion, and authenticity in all we do—to cultivate deep connections with ourselves, others, and the world around us.

As we step forward into this new beginning, let us do so with courage, curiosity, and an unwavering commitment to living our lives with passion, purpose, and presence. Let us remember that we are the architects of our own destiny, and that the power to create the life of our dreams lies within each and every one of us. And let us never forget that we are not alone on this journey—that we are supported, guided, and held by the boundless love and wisdom of the universe.

In closing, I extend my deepest gratitude to you, dear reader, for accompanying me on this journey of exploration and discovery. May the wisdom contained within these pages serve as a beacon of light on your path, illuminating the way forward as you continue your own journey of self-discovery, transformation, and mystic love. And may you always remember that the greatest adventure of all is the journey of the heart—a journey that leads us ever closer to the truth of who we are and the boundless love that lies at the very core of our being.

Thank you for buying and reading/ listening to our book. If you found this book useful/ helpful please take a few minutes and leave a review on the platform where you purchased our book. Your feedback matters greatly to us.

www.ingramcontent.com/pod-product-compliance
Lightning Source LLC
LaVergne TN
LVHW051952060526
838201LV00059B/3605